The Joy of Jesus

The Joy of Jesus

Humour in the Gospels

Richard Buckner

The Canterbury Press
Norwich

First published 1993 by The Canterbury Press Norwich
(a publishing imprint of Hymns Ancient & Modern Limited,
a registered charity)
St Mary's Works, St Mary's Plain,
Norwich, Norfolk, NR3 3BH

A catalogue record for this book is available
from the British Library

ISBN 1–85311–067–1

*Photoset by Rowland Phototypesetting Limited,
Bury St Edmunds, Suffolk
and printed in Great Britain by
St Edmundsbury Press Limited,
Bury St Edmunds, Suffolk*

PUBLISHER'S NOTE

Richard Buckner was born in Totnes in 1937. From Kelly College, Tavistock in Devon, he went to Keble College, Oxford, from 1957 to 1960. He married Anne in 1960 and went to Wells Theological College. After ordination he served his title at Crediton. Later, while a curate at St Matthew's, Exeter he took up part-time teaching and obtained his teacher's certificate at St Luke's, Exeter. In 1966 he was appointed Chaplain to Grenville College, Bideford. Nine years later he went to Worksop College, Notts, and in 1982 he became Chaplain at Merchant Taylors', Northwood. It was in 1991, only one term after taking up an appointment at Gresham's, Holt, that Richard Buckner died of asthma, an illness that had plagued him ever since he was a child. Besides leaving a wife and two sons and two daughters, he has left behind examples of his great sense of humour. The typescript for this book, completed before his death, reached us via the Bishop of Norwich, from the author's widow.

Included at the end of the book are a number of examples of the author's verse, written under the pen name of 'Avery Goodman'. Illustrations are by the author's great friend Phil Densham.

Bible quotations are taken from the New English Bible, 1970 © Oxford & Cambridge University Presses.

Contents

THE JOY OF JESUS

Introduction

THE GOSPELS provide abundant material which, when discovered, radiates Christ's joyful personality. From this emerges an interpretation of his life which may have a far-reaching effect on our own personal commitment. Christian joy is there for all to see, but centuries of emphasis on the dogmatic and penitential aspect of the Christian Faith have dulled the simple, cheerful life-style which our Lord followed.

A careful and perceptive study of the Synoptic Gospels, and to a certain extent St John's, will show us that Jesus used various types of humour, ranging from absolute absurdity to subtle irony, from riddles to amusing parables.

As every teacher knows, humour plays an essential part of 'getting over' to pupils, young and old alike. Jesus had a vital message for men and women. It was the call to a New Life. 'The Kingdom of God is upon you; repent, and believe the Gospel.' The Good News *is* Christ. A time for rejoicing. A time of faithful happiness. A time of good humour.

Cardinal Francois Marty of Paris, commenting on the brief reign of Pope John Paul I, said:

> 'The Pope had a message to give the world. He gave us the smile of God. In the greyness of these days, this smile will remain like a beam of light.'

Jesus himself was the first to give us the smile of God. The smile that radiates good humour, compassion, fellowship, serenity, and love. This is the joy of the Gospel. This is the Good News for today's world.

Chapter 1

In search of happiness

FOR MANY people, young and old, life is a constant striving after happiness. 'Enjoy yourself – it's later than you think!' cries the modern Epicurean, and amid the frustrations and disappointments of life he often achieves moments of pleasure. This may last for a while, but it doesn't come from the depth of his personality. It is only on the surface. Another tension soon reveals this 'happiness' as shallow and superficial. It doesn't come from the heart.

It is one of the peculiarities of the Christian Way of Life that the goal of happiness in its deepest and most realistic sense can only be reached through self-sacrifice and service. Modern man throws up his hands in dismay. How on earth can I be happy if I stop thinking about myself? How can I enjoy life if I give up personal ambitions and pleasures? Without self-esteem and self-gratification there's no fun in life! There's no sense in that unless you enjoy being miserable!

Christ's words known as the Beatitudes from the 'Sermon on the Mount' (Matt.5.3ff) lay down the code for Christian happiness. How blest are the humble, the sympathetic, the unselfish, the merciful, the sincere, those who make peace, and those who suffer for Christ's sake. These are the sort of people who will gain joyful fulfilment in life, not superficially and occasionally, but in depth. This is the personality of Christ himself which radiates through the pages of the Gospels. And it is this aspect of the life of Christ which has always been the most neglected, even denied. So the Good News has lost its joy, and Christ's radiance has been dulled.

Children seldom look upon our Lord as a cheerful person. They seem to think he was either a grave and strict teacher, bent on fulfilling his mission to turn to God sinners like old Uncle Charlie who is always drunk come Saturday night, or a gentle, almost harmless prophet who suffered on a cross because he let his enemies take him without a fight. These childish impressions often last until the young adult rejects them – and the Christian Faith as well. There is nothing in this man's personality which attracts. No inspiration. No point of contact. Meaningless.

Cheerful disposition

And yet when we read the Acts of the Apostles (notably 2.42–47) we see how Christ's followers were renowned for their cheerful disposition. They weren't a morbid bunch frustrated and embittered by the failure of their leader. Far from it! They were fired with Christ's enthusiasm for a life dedicated to God at every point. Here for all to see was the joy of the Resurrection. This transparent happiness showed how much their faith meant to them, and many who were attracted by this outward joy soon learned its inward reason. Here was the mark of their deep assurance of the love of God and a reflection of the person of Christ. Real joy: a gift of the Holy Spirit. This happiness added a new dimension to life in the first century AD (see Luke 24.52; Acts 8.8;13.52; Rom. 12.12;14.17;15.13; Phil. 3.1;4.4; 1 Thess. 5.16; 1 Peter 1.6–8; 1 John 1.3–4; et alia).

Undoubtedly Christ himself manifested this joy in his cheerful approach to life. There are many examples of this, often unrecognised, in the Gospel narratives. Readers of the New Testament are aware of Christ's solemnity and his humility, but these characteristics are not likely to have drawn to him crowds who 'hung on his every word'.

In the Old Testament joy is the inward and outward expression of a conscious nearness to God. This is particularly noticeable in the Psalms (see 4.7; 5.11; 16.11; 28.7; 32.11; 51.12; 63.7; 68.3; 89.16; 97.11,12; 100.2; et alia). This feeling of exultation became connected with the growing expectation of God's revelation. Naturally this is carried over into the New Testament. Now the Kingdom of God *is* at hand, and there is great joy in the Good News which Jesus announces. Jesus projects this joy through his healing and teaching.

If he was a severe and unsmiling Saviour there would be little joy in his revelation of God's Kingdom. It was his nearness to God which reflected the joy: and this inner happiness over-bubbled in cheerfulness and good humour. Not superficial happiness turned on at the right moment. A permanent happiness based on God's love from the depth of his person. His Spirit: God's Spirit.

For centuries Christians have devoutly read the Gospels without enjoying much of what Jesus said. They have failed to notice the twinkle in Christ's eye and haven't heard the gaiety in his voice.

The events of Holy Week have formed the centre of the Gospel tradition. Not much light relief here. And once the theologians took hold of the life of Christ his personality faded into dogma. The Christian message of joy and hope, so apparent in the Early Church, disappeared into centuries of guilt-ridden fear and obsession with orthodoxy.

How often do we smile when we read the Gospels? Perhaps Christ's amusing remarks don't seem so funny today, but against the background of first century Palestine they must have often made his listeners laugh.

This was all part of his warm good-naturedness which attracted people to him. He was also capable of pitting his wits against the self-righteous Pharisees who took life so desperately seriously.

And he was a brilliant story-teller. Small wonder those who heard him remembered the parables he told them and his off-the-cuff repartee.

The Church, by failing to see the smile on Christ's face and to hear the light-hearted tone of his voice, has lost the joyfulness of the Good News. The Gospel, for many people, has become dull and meaningless. This was the experience of the late John Moore who some years ago gave his Opinion in what was then the *Weekend Telegraph* supplement under the heading 'Why must Christians be so miserable?'

'My earliest recollections of church-going concern my bewilderment that although you might feel happy, you had to pretend to be sad. I remember watching how the smiles on people's faces were extinguished by some power-cut of the spirit as they came to the church porch, how they all wore the same miserable expressions as they went up the aisle. I found this all the more strange because I was a happy child. I see buttercups shining in the sun: I hear the distant roar of the Severn Weir, and have an undefined, thrilling sense of adventure, delight in discovery, in living. Across the meadow I see the great tower of Tewkesbury Abbey, glowing in the sun. But whenever I went inside that abbey, there was a chill which struck at my spirit as well as my body, all was gloom and hush, all about me was solemnity. . . . To me the world was not miserable, but was beautiful and exciting. The people I knew were on the whole kindly and good: the idea of all-pervading sinfulness made no sense at all . . .

It has been put to me since, that what I took to be the misery of Christian worship was no more than a proper sense of awe of the majesty and mystery of God. But I was far more aware of God's majesty in high mountains, a raging sea or wild weather, and later through poetry, than I ever felt in church.

My young agnosticism stemmed from this: I could not believe in a God who preferred solemn faces to cheerful ones, gravity to laughter, misery to joy . . .

I am not an atheist, for I can discover divinity in everything that lifts my spirit or delights my sense. If there is a God, then surely he must manifest himself in lovely things, in the primrose and the poem: the leaping salmon and the galloping horse: in pretty girls, wine, butterflies, buttercups, swift waters, sunset skies, in Beethoven and Shakespeare: above all in the human spirit – its tenderness in love, its imagination and its daring, its happiness and sorrow.'*

Surely God, the giver of all these innumerable blessings, is a God of happiness and joy: the Father whom Jesus by his life and death revealed to mankind?

Jesus preached about the Kingdom of God, a new spiritual dimension to life, and this was the Good News. This joyfulness was radiated through his person by what he did and said.

* John Moore *Weekend Telegraph* 16.4.66. See also Joachim Kahl *The Misery of Christianity* (Penguin, 1971)

Chapter 2

Make 'em laugh!

I ONCE conducted a survey in a rural Comprehensive school to find out what the senior pupils reckoned was the quality most desired in their boy/girl friends. Unanimous answer: a sense of humour, a cheerful disposition. I have seen this opinion expressed on numerous occasions since then. We all enjoy having someone around who amuses and cheers us up. It isn't a matter of cracking jokes all the time like the over-paid so-called comics of the entertainment world. (What are they *really* like?) There are often people around who are *naturally* far more amusing than the professionals.

Laughter is conditioned by one's sense of humour. It is a personal response. Much depends on the situation and the individual's awareness and appreciation of what is amusing. Types of humour change. A quick look at a Victorian *Punch* demonstrates this. It is often difficult to understand the humour of different countries.

However, there are some universal types of humour, and there are examples of these in the Gospel narratives. Christ uses various forms of figurative speech – hyperbole, metaphor, simile – riddles, plays-on-words, witty rejoinders, irony, teasing and banter, catchphrases, symbolism, and friendly ridicule, plus, of course, his own particular brand of story-telling and colourful illustration (cp. John 16.25).

Somehow much of this humour has been lost. It may be due to over-familiarity with the text or to translation from Greek or original Aramaic. Unfortunately the main reason seems to be that religion has always been considered a serious subject, and consequently there is little, if any, place for humour in it. The pharisaic approach is still with us.

The process of de-humourising Christ can be seen as soon as we depart from his original words. The form critics have probably drawn our attention to this, although their lack of imagination and disregard for rabbinical teaching methods have led them to make rather negative assumptions about the authenticity of many of Christ's sayings. The writers of the Synoptic Gospels reveal, perhaps unwittingly sometimes, the good-naturedness of our Lord, but lose it once they start to add their own material, probably under the influence of the Early Church and contemporary practice. St Paul is very conscious of the joy of the Resurrection, but he took his theology very seriously, and there is little sparkle in his extant writings.

St John, writing sometime later, in his inspired interpretation of the life of Christ, while tending to theologise in long discourses – no parables, no witticism – does occasionally suggest that he has experienced the joyfulness that inspired Jesus' first disciples.

> 'I have spoken this to you,
> so that my joy may be in you,
> and your joy complete'
>
> (John 15.11)

> 'For the moment you are sad at heart;
> but I shall see you again,
> and then you will be joyful,
> and no one shall rob you of your joy'
>
> (John 16.22)

> 'And now I am coming to thee:
> but while I am still in the world
> I speak these words,
> so that they may have my joy within them in full measure'
>
> (John 17.13)

The NEB translation retains the hint of a rhythm in these inspired utterances, a traditional characteristic of prophetical and rabbinical speech.

Every teacher knows that humour is often an ideal method of instruction. An amusing story or a comic verse will always be remembered. So will a wise, catchy saying or a subtle pun.

Jesus was dealing with people who were accustomed to use their imaginations and commit what they heard to memory. No cassettes or action replays then. So he followed the practice of the Jewish rabbis and brought it to perfection. We can be confident that much of the Gospel material in which there is a touch of humour is the authentic teaching of our Lord. It is individualistic and inimitable. It appealed to those who had 'ears to hear' and was easily remembered. It was the cheerful extension of his personality. Here was the Good News in action.

Instead of condemning sinners he laughed with them, not at them. He chided the Pharisees, teasing them with stories of vanity and hypocrisy. He ridiculed the priests for their pomposity and arrogant piety. The crowds who flocked to hear him must have loved it. He even had fun with his own disciples, although they didn't always realise it.

Sense of humour

As we read the first three Gospels we should be on the look-out for occasions which reveal Jesus' sense of humour. Well loved passages may be seen in a new light: fresh understanding of a difficult verse may be gained by the injection of some humour into it. We should visualise the saying or incident in our own mind. Imagine the picture Jesus is drawing. Notice the amusing caricatures, the flashes of wit, the punch-lines. In our own mind's eye see how Jesus punctures the Pharisees' self-righteousness, points the truth by presenting the absurd and grotesque, states the obvious, confuses the lawyers and scribes, turns the tables on his opponents, teases his disciples, and especially picture his marvellous stories. And then, with a rueful smile perhaps, we may apply what Jesus teaches to ourselves.

Recent scholarship has revealed the probability of an Aramaic sayings source behind the Gospels. Jesus, of course, spoke Aramaic with a Galilean accent – similar to the local dialects of any country. Likewise Peter, who when denying that he knew Christ gave himself away because of his accent (Matt. 26.73).

Modern translations may lose much of the Aramaic idioms, and especially the popular poetic form and rhythm, so easy to commit to memory, which Jesus would have used. And yet, the original Aramaic still shines through, particularly in the areas of Christ's humour. This is particularly noticeable in his use of Semitic parallelism. A few examples may be more helpful than an explanation.

> 'Whoever then will *acknowledge me before* men,
> I will *acknowledge him before* my Father in heaven;
> and whosoever *disowns me before* men,
> I will *disown him before* my Father in heaven.'
>
> (Matt. 10.32,33)

> 'Whoever *receives* one of these children in my name, *receives* me;
> and whoever *receives* me,
> *receives* not me but the one who sent me.'
>
> (Mark 9.37; cp. Matt. 10.40f.)

> 'For nothing is hidden unless it is to be disclosed, and nothing put under cover unless it is to come into the open.'
>
> (Mark 4.22)

The collection of Christ's sayings under the heading of the Sermon on the Mount abound with poetic parallelisms.

> 'Do not suppose that *I have come to abolish*
> the Law and the prophets;
> *I do not come to abolish*,
> but to complete.'
>
> (Matt. 5.17)

> 'A good tree always yields good fruit,
> and a poor tree bad fruit.
> A good tree cannot bear bad fruit,
> or a poor tree good fruit.'
>
> (Matt. 7.17,18)

'Ask, and you will receive;
seek, and you will find;
knock, and the door will be opened.
For everyone who asks receives,
he who seeks finds,
and to him who knocks, the door will be opened.'

(Matt. 7.7,8)

And there are many more. All so easy to commit to memory –
like parables, puns, riddles, and all the other figures of speech
which our Lord used to win his audience.

The examples that follow are not exhaustive. They are
merely intended to point the way to a re-appraisal of some of
the recorded words of Jesus which suggest, at least to me, that
our Lord had a marvellous sense of humour.

Chapter 3

Jesus and John the Baptist

THIS PASSAGE from Luke 7.31–35 gives a clear indication of Jesus' cheerful character.

> 'How can I describe the people of this generation?
> What are they like?
> They are like children sitting in the market-place and shouting at each other,
> "We piped for you and you would not dance."
> "We wept and wailed, and you would not mourn."
> For John the Baptist came neither eating bread nor drinking wine,
> and you say, "He is possessed."
> The Son of Man came eating and drinking,
> and you say, "Look at him! a glutton and a drinker, a friend of tax-gatherers and sinners!"
> And yet God's wisdom is proved right by all who are her children.'

John the Baptist, now imprisoned, sent two of his disciples to make some discreet enquiries about Jesus.

> 'Are you the one who is to come,
> or are we to expect some other?'

Like many others, John was puzzled by the course events were taking. Aware that his own life was in dagner he longed to see Jesus, the one for whom he had prepared the way, revealed and acknowledged as God's Messiah.

Jesus did not answer these questions. Instead he let John's

messengers see him at work among the sick, the devil-possessed, and the disabled, and left them to form their own conclusions.

When John's disciples have gone Jesus asks the crowd about the Baptist (Luke 7.24,25). There must have been a twinkle in his eye when he asked,

> 'What was the spectacle that drew you to the wilderness?
> A reed-bed swept by the wind?
> No? Then what did you go out to see?
> A man dressed in silks and satins?
> Surely you must look in palaces for grand clothes and luxury!'

Can you imagine a ripple of laughter running through the crowd after each question? Who would venture into the wilderness to see a reed-bed swept by the wind – or a man dressed in silks and satins!

The final punch-line demonstrates Christ's use of irony; not cynical, but good-natured banter; a little 'dig' at the aristocracy.

Jesus acknowledges his indebtedness to John: here was a prophet in the Old Testament style, but so much more than that.

> 'Here is my herald, whom I send on ahead of you,
> And he will prepare your way before you.'
>
> (Luke 7.27)

Many people had accepted John's Baptism, but the Pharisees and lawyers had refused. John had appealed to the Jewish man-in-the-street, but his message had been rejected by the religious leaders. Self-absorbed, self-righteous, and self-confident, they could make little sense of either John or Jesus.

In contrasting their life-styles, Jesus reveals the very different personalities of John and himself. He describes that people generally are like children who get cross when others won't play their games. When John appeared out of the wilderness, austere and ascetic, dressed in rough clothes – not in silks and satins – they wanted him to sing and dance, to show himself more human, to be 'one of the chaps'.* When he refused to play their game they accused him of 'being possessed', 'a wierdo'.*

When Jesus came with joy and conviviality they were some-what shocked and thought that He should be more serious and aloof. They accused Him of being 'a glutton and a drinker, a friend of tax-gatherers and sinners'. He was too human!

Both John and Jesus were fulfilling God's purpose and interpreting their lives according to his Will. But it is clear from the above that neither life-style satisfied the critics. You just can't win. And today, inside and outside the Church, there are many believers and non-believers who are equally hard to please!

It is in the striking contrast between John and Jesus that we glimpse, or perhaps see clearly, the cheerful, amusing side of Christ's personality. John prepared the way for Jesus to announce,

> 'The Kingdom of God is upon you;
> repent, and believe the Gospel.'
>
> (Mark 1.15)

Here was the call to a New Life. A time for rejoicing. Deer happiness. 'Be of good cheer.' And Jesus had plenty of it.

I remember being in a parish in Devon where the vicar was a tall, clean-shaven, aloof-looking man; he took life seriously. People said he was out of touch. In a neighbouring parish was his exact opposite; a squat, bearded priest, warm personality, who raced around the narrow Devon lanes visiting the locals. They said he spent too much time in the pub.

You can't please everyone! Both men had the right qualities. The first, contemplative, scholarly, a man devoted to the Church: the second, outward-going, concerned for the lost, a man of action.

---

*Colloquial expressions (not drawn from Scripture).

Chapter 4
Jesus v Pharisees

IT IS in his clashes with the Pharisees that we get numerous amusing examples of Christ's sense of humour. It isn't sarcasm – that is designed to hurt. More likely, whimsical ridicule; a gentle 'dig'.

There were other occasions when he was outspoken, but he never intended to be spiteful, to belittle, or to show contempt, I'm sure of that. To appreciate our Lord's exchanges it is necessary to know something about the Pharisees.

In the first century BC the Hasidaeans were the fanatical supporters of the Jewish Law which they loyally upheld against all foreign 'progressive' influences. They endeavoured to apply the Law to every aspect of life, and consequently developed a mass of regulations down to the pettiest of details. The Pharisees were the immediate successors of the Hasidim. Their scribes and lawyers were the 'experts' who interpreted the inherited Law of Moses (Torah) – on occasions to suit their own position. Sometimes these 'interpretations' even contradicted the original Law (Mark 7.9–13).

The name 'Pharisees' means 'separate ones', i.e. God's faithful people who have separated themselves from the world. This exclusiveness had the effect of making the Pharisees aloof, self-righteous, and unsympathetic to the humble efforts and failings of anyone else. This bigotted attitude was an ideal target for Christ's quick-witted ripostes, especially as the Pharisees appear to have taken themselves, oh, so seriously.

Jesus astounded them by his new lifestyle. He ate with sinners, tax-gatherers and the like! Jesus explained why,

'It is not the healthy that need a doctor, but the sick.
I did not come to invite virtuous people, but sinners.'
(Mark 2.15–17)

Memorable words not easily forgotten. Matthew adds that on this occasion (Matt. 9.13) and again later Matt. 12.7) Jesus referred the Pharisees to the well-known Old Testament text (Hosea 6.6).

'I require mercy, not sacrifice.' Instead of fasting with his disciples, Jesus took them to parties. On the sabbath he scandalised his critics on several recorded occasions. When his disciples were accused of plucking corn – 'harvesting' according to the interpretation of the Law – he questioned the Pharisees' knowledge of the sacred Scriptures at which they were experts, and added,

'The Sabbath was made for the sake of man and not man for the Sabbath.'

(Mark 2.23–27)

A notable comment or aphorism which not even his opponents would forget in a hurry (verse 28 is probably a later addition, maybe by the Evangelist). On the next occasion Jesus finds a man with a withered arm in the synagogue. Luke records that the Pharisees watched to see if our Lord would heal him on the Sabbath. Jesus confronts them with a disarming question,

'If one of you has a donkey or an ox
and it falls into a well,
will he hesitate to haul it up
on the Sabbath day?'

(Luke 14.1–6)

No reply.

Matthew's version is a little different. Probably recalled from a similar situation. Same feigned surprise.

'If one of you has a donkey or an ox
and it falls into a well,
will he hesitate to haul it up
on the Sabbath day?'

17

'And surely a man is worth more than a sheep?'

'Suppose you had one sheep, which fell into a ditch on the Sabbath;
is there one of you who would not catch hold of it and lift it out?'

And then Jesus adds his punch-line,

'And surely a man is worth far more than a sheep!'
(Matthew 12.9–14)

Mark tells us that Jesus was angry (3.5), and doesn't mention the pertinent questions. Even His good humour may have evaporated sometimes.

Most small children brought up in the health-conscious society of the twentieth century will have been encouraged to wash their hands before meals. They may, therefore, appreciate to some extent Christ's confrontation with the Pharisees on the matter of defilement – ritualistic rather than hygienic. The Pharisees were so concerned about their 'inner cleanliness' that they took meticulous care not to eat or drink anything that might contaminate or defile them. Hence their fastidiousness in washing themselves and their utensils before a meal. It had become quite a performance! Jesus explains that real religious purity is found in a person's heart: it isn't a question of unclean food entering a person – that goes right through him . . .

'Do you not see that nothing that goes from outside into a man can defile him,
because it does not enter into his heart but into his stomach,
and so passes out into the drain?'
(Mark 7.19, Matt.15.17)

I wonder what the Puritans made of this down-to-earth remark!

Jesus did not condemn the observances, but clearly showed that they had become all out of proportion, to the neglect of things which really matter. Concern for minute details of ritual had taken the place of real religious faith and worship (cf. Matt. 23.25,26). Both Matthew and Luke while narrating the above include Christ's 'dig' at the Pharisaic practice of occasionally manipulating the Law to suit their own ends. He instances 'Corban' – a clever dodge whereby a son, instead of supporting his parents, can dedicate his earnings to the Temple, and probably use the money for himself.

Having witnessed many of Christ's recorded miracles – and, no doubt, many more besides – the Pharisees press him to show them a sign from heaven. In Mark 8.11–13 Jesus refuses, but in Matthew 16.1–4 and Luke 12.54–56 he refers his inquirers to the weather forecast in the sky. If they can interpret the weather, they ought to be able to read the signs of the times!

Christ's reference to the sign of Jonah should remind his hearers that it was Jonah who preached repentance to the citizens of Nineveh – and they repented. The contrast is clear. At least, the Pharisees would see it.

Jesus' warning about the 'leaven' of the Pharisees follows immediately in Matthew and Mark (cf. Luke 12.1). Matthew interprets it as their teaching, Luke as hypocrisy, and Mark leaves the word-play alone.

The Pharisees were so self-confident that their arrogance blinded them. They observed the faults of others, but not their own. They observed the letter of the Law, but failed to see its fulfilment in Christ.

> 'Blind Pharisee!
> Clean the inside of the cup first;
> then the outside will be clean also.'
>
> (Matt. 23.26, cf. Luke 11.37ff.)

When Christ's disciples report that the Pharisees have been offended by what he said – a regular sequel? – Jesus replies flippantly,

> 'Leave them alone;
> they are blind guides,
> and if one blind man guides another
> they will both fall into the ditch.'
>
> (Matt. 15.14, cp. Luke 6.39)

'They are blind guides,
and if one blind man guides another
they will both fall into the ditch.'

In John 8.12 the writer of the fourth Gospel contrasts the light and darkness of the world.

> 'I am the light of the world.
> No follower of mine shall wander in the dark;
> he shall have the light of life.'

John continues the theme of 'blindness' in chapter 9.
The Pharisees ask, 'Do you mean that we are blind?'

> 'If you were blind,' said Jesus,
> 'you would not be guilty,
> but because you say "We see",
> your guilt remains.'
>
> (John 9.40,41)

Spiritual blindness is often the outcome of overemphasis on man-made rules and regulations. Impersonality is bred by faceless bureaucracy and 'red tape'.

In the Sermon on the Mount Jesus was probably thinking of the Pharisees when he said,

> 'Be careful not to make a show of your religion before men . . .'
>
> (Matt. 6.1)

In Matthew 23 Jesus warns his hearers about them. This whole section has been edited by the Evangelist, but it is still possible to detect glimpses of genuine sayings of Christ, particularly the humorous ones.

> 'They go about with broad phylacteries* and with large tassels on their robes.'
>
> (v.5, cf. Matt. 6.1)

---

*Texts written on parchment and worn hanging from the wrist, like an amulet to ward off evil spirits. So Jesus describes them as 'charms'!

'You shut the door of the kingdom of Heaven [God] in men's faces.'

(v.13)

'Blind guides!
You strain off a midge,
yet gulp down a camel!'

(v.24)

'You shut the door of the kingdom of Heaven in men's faces.'

'You are like tombs covered with whitewash;
they look well from outside,
but inside they are full of dead
men's bones and all kinds of filth.'

(v.27, cf. Luke 11.44)

Ostentation in prayer is lampooned by Jesus in this famous
caricature:

'They love to say their prayers
standing up in synagogue
and at the street-corners,
for everyone to see.'

(Matt. 6.5)

Jesus amplifies this in a short parable which Luke alone
records. It is aimed, we are told, at those who are sure of their
own goodness and look down on everyone else (cf. Matt. 5.20).

As in most parables, Jesus allows himself a little exaggera-
tion to add humour and colour in order to make the point of his
story more memorable.

A Pharisee and tax-gatherer go up to the Temple to pray. The
Pharisee prays, in his self-righteous way,

'I thank thee, O God, that I am not like the rest of men,
greedy, dishonest, adulterous; or, for that matter, like
this tax-gatherer . . .'

In contrast the latter, showing true humility and repentance,
prays,

'O God, have mercy on me,
sinner that I am.'

(Luke 18.9–14)

The lesson of Christ's story is clear: the caricature fits both
men.

Luke demonstrates the contrast between the self-
righteousness of the Pharisees and the love and forgiveness

of sinners by Jesus. In 7.36–50, the incident of the notorious woman washing our Lord's feet, Luke has taken Mark 14.3–9 (Matt. 26.6–13) and recast it to illustrate the same theme as that of the Prodigal Son – Christ's forgiveness.

Jesus does not condemn sinners – like the Pharisees – nor does he condone.

> 'Is it easier to say to this paralysed man,
> "Your sins are forgiven", or to say,
> "Stand up, take your bed, and walk"?'
>
> (Mark 2.1–12)

Jesus may have been aggravated by the attitude of the Pharisees – exaggerated piety and hypocrisy have a distasteful effect on most people – but it is unlikely that he attacked them with as much vigour as the Gospel narratives suggest. Many Pharisees made a real effort to follow the Law of Moses and to enjoy a relationship with their Creator. They may have been misguided, but Jesus would not condemn them for that.

On various occasions Jesus called them 'hypocrites' – the Greek word meaning 'play-actors' (see Matt. 15.7; 16.3; 22.18, esp. chapter 23; Mark 7.6; Luke 11.44; 12.1 and 56; 13.15).

They were putting on an act. Jesus could see into men's hearts and knew what they were really like. He didn't condemn them – just let them see that he could read them. It may have been a light-hearted title. Ridicule is a means of teaching, not necessarily unkind.

Chapter 5

Absurdities

NOWADAYS 'elephant jokes' are popular, their appeal lying in the total absurdity of the situation depicted, e.g.

> How do you know if there's an elephant hiding in the fridge?
> You can't shut the door.
>
> Why don't elephants climb trees?
> They can't stand heights.

An elephant may look an ungainly animal, but it doesn't have the grotesqueness of the camel. 'Camel jokes' may have been 'in' when Jesus was around. There are two examples in the Gospels.

In his inspiring book *The Jesus of History*, written as long ago as 1916, T. R. Glover draws attention to Christ's use of humour and instances his absurd picture of the Pharisee's meticulous care before drinking.* Leviticus 11.41ff forbade the eating of anything that swarmed or crept on the earth, and so the devout Jew strained everything he drank. Jesus is criticising the lawyers and Pharisees for their concern for paying tithes . . .

> '. . . but you have overlooked
> the weightier demands of the Law,
> justice, mercy, and good faith.
> It is these you should have practised,

---

*See also Jesus' teaching on defilement p. 19.

without neglecting the others.
Blind guides!
You strain off a midge, yet gulp down a camel.'

(Matt. 23.23,24)

Glover draws out the ridiculous details of this amusing caricature of the Pharisee's minute preparations before drinking his
wine: a picture which Christ's original listeners would have
drawn in their minds, and, no doubt, they would have chuckled
to themselves as they realised its utter absurdity.

Have you ever thought what swallowing a camel would look
like? All good Monty Python humour which would have
delighted anyone in the crowd with a reasonable imagination.

> 'We are shown the man polishing his cup, elaborately
> and carefully; for he lays great importance on the
> cleanness of his cup; but he forgets to clean the inside.
> Most people drink from the inside, but the Pharisee
> forgot it, dirty as it was, and left it untouched. Then he
> sets about straining what he is going to drink – another
> elaborate process; he holds a piece of muslin over the
> cup and pours with care; he pauses – he sees a
> mosquito; he has caught it in time and flicks it away; he
> is safe and will not swallow it. And then, adds Jesus, he
> swallowed a camel! How many of us have ever pictured
> the process, and the series of sensations, as the long
> hairy neck slid down the throat of the Pharisee – all that
> amplitude of loose-hung anatomy – the hump – two
> humps – both of them slid down – and he never noticed
> it – and the legs – all of them – with whole outfit of
> knees and big padded feet. The Pharisee swallowed a
> camel – and never noticed it (Matt. 23.24,25). Did no
> one smile as the story was told? Did no one see the scene
> pictured with his own mind's eye – no one grasp the
> humour and the irony with delight? It is the mixture of
> sheer realism with absurdity that makes the irony and
> gives it such force. A modern teacher would have said,
> in our jargon, that the Pharisee had no sense of propor-

tion – and no one would have thought the remark worth remembering'.*

The Pharisees were so concerned with the petty details of the Law that they overlooked the vital demands of justice, mercy, and good faith.

And now for the second 'camel joke'. A rich (young) man comes to Jesus to ask how he can win eternal life. He has kept all the commandments faithfully since he was a boy. Jesus tells him to sell everything he has – and his heart sinks. Jesus says,

> 'How hard it is for the wealthy to enter the Kingdom of God. *It is easier for a camel to go through the eye of a needle* than for a rich man to enter the Kingdom of God.'
>
> (Luke 18.18–27, Mark 10.25)

An example of Jesus' use of hyperbole, an exaggerated statement, which has been blurred by attempts to explain the saying in some other way. There is no evidence that there was a very small gate in Jerusalem called 'the Needle's Eye' – although Holy Land guides may have 'discovered' one. Nor is there any reason for suggesting that *camelos* (camel) is a mistranslation of *camilos* (cable or piece of camel's hair).

The ingenuity of these attempts are almost as amusing as the original remark – an exaggerated expression easily remembered by its vivid absurdity which, despite its humour, stresses a serious aspect of man's commitment to God, namely, that you cannot serve God and Money.

No wonder people remembered Jesus' teaching and hung on his words. In the Gospels there are only the two examples of our Lord's 'camel jokes', but it is likely that he used this butt of ridicule many times to gain the attention of his audience and to give all his listeners a light-hearted reminder of a serious aspect of life. Insensitive to a camel's feelings? Well, have you ever seen an unhappy camel? Surely the most resilient and philo-

*Quoted from T. R. Glover *The Jesus of History*, by kind permission of SCM Press.

'When you do an act of charity,
do not announce it with a flourish of trumpets.'

sophical of beats of burden. They probably appreciated Christ's fun-poking.

The Gospels clearly reveal how Jesus often deliberately exaggerated a point to impress his hearers. No one who heard the original version of Matt. 7.3–5 is likely to forget the absurd imagery.

> 'Why do you look at the *speck of sawdust* in your brother's eye, with never a thought for the *great plank* in your own?'

What a vivid hyperbole, and what an absurd, but memorable, picture it conjures up.

> 'Or how can you say to your brother,
> "Let me take the speck out of your eye",
> when all the time there is
> *that plank* in your own?'

The perfect illustration of a hypocrite: not a careful definition, but an amusing caricature, easily kept in mind.

Another absurd example of a hypocrite concerns his ostentation when performing an act of charity.

> 'Thus, when you do some act of charity, do not announce it with a *flourish of trumpets*,
> as the hypocrites do in synagogue
> and in the streets
> to win the admiration of men.'
>
> (Matt. 6.2)

A preposterous remark, of course, but not without a certain measure of truth. Most people like to be known for their generosity.

No one in their right minds is likely to feed pearls to pigs. Jesus warns his listeners to discriminate between the worthy and the unworthy: do not devalue what is holy by association with godless people. no wonder 'pearls before swine' is a well-known figure of speech today.

'Do not feed your pearls to pigs.'

'Do not give *dogs* what is *holy*;
do not feed your *pearls* to *pigs*:
they will only trample on them,
and turn and tear you to pieces.'

(Matt. 7.6)

Again, Jesus makes a serious point in an amusing way. And his Jewish audience had a pretty low opinion of pigs and dogs; they were terms of abuse.

Jesus emphasises the power of fiath with one of his typical hyperboles. Faith no bigger than a mustard-seed is sufficient 'to move mountains'. Our Lord here uses a Jewish expression, a metaphor referring to something very difficult (Mark 11.23; Matt. 17.20). Luke prefers 'mulberry-tree' to 'mountain'. Jesus again stresses the power of faith, obviously aware that the sycomore (no, not sycamore) had deep roots, and therefore to transplant it in the sea was even more impressive (Luke 17.5,6).

As an introduction to the Parable of the Unforgiving Servant Matthew prefaces a question from Peter about forgiveness. How often should one forgive his brother? Seven times?

Jesus by overstating makes it clear that forgiveness is never-ending.

'I do not say seven times;
I say *seventy* times seven.'

(Matt. 18.21,22)

Jesus sounds particularly vehement when he warns against leading others astray.

'As for the man who is a cause of stumbling to one of these little ones who have faith, it would be better for him to be thrown into the sea with a *millstone round his neck.*'

(Mark 9.42; Matt. 18.6; Luke 17.2)

That's the way to deal with the corrupters of the young. It may sound far-fetched, but it makes the point. Likewise, Christ's

*'It would be better for him
to be thrown into the sea
with a millstone round his neck!'*

following advice about personal inclination to sin . . .

> 'If your hand is your undoing, cut it off;
> it is better for you to enter into life maimed
> than to keep both hands and go to hell*
> and the unquenchable fire . . .'

Jesus goes on to add that an errant foot should be cut off and a lustful eye torn out (Mark 9.43ff; Matt. 5.29; 18.8). This may sound rather macabre, but it stresses the gravity of personal error and suggests a solution, however painful.

Those present would have remembered Christ's quick retort to one of his disciples who asked,

> 'Lord, let me go and bury my father first.'

Jesus replied,

> 'Follow me,
> and leave the dead to bury their dead.'
>
> (Matt. 8.21,22; Luke 9.60)

There are different interpretations of this particular passage, and Christ's reply is probably not as callous as it sounds. He may, perhaps, be playing on the word 'dead', meaning those who are spiritually dead.

Readers of the Gospels should be aware that a touch of humour often illuminates a difficult translation, and passages which appear to be bordering on the ridiculous may be clearly understood if our Lord's use of hyperbole is acknowledged.

---

*Probably the valley west of Jerusalem used as the city refuse tip. Gehenna, with its earlier associations with child sacrifice and its stinking and smoking refuse, had come to be regarded as the place of future torment.

Chapter 6

Stating the obvious

'If a man walks on hot coals,
will his feet not be scorched?'

(Proverbs 6.28)

THERE IS a certain amount of humour in stating the obvious. It often suggests that the speaker is underestimating the IQ of his audience and therefore has to keep his statements simple and clear-cut. Perhaps Jesus was merely concerned to emphasise the simple truth, although Galilean fishermen may have been rather similar to the once much ridiculed Irish labourers.

There are several examples of obvious statements in the collection of Christ's sayings under the heading of 'The Sermon on the Mount'. This is not the place to discuss the editorial additions to Christ's words. It seems more likely that where there is a trace of humour we are dealing with authentic material.

When Jesus wishes to impress upon his disciples their responsibility to 'spread the Gospel' he says,

'You are light for all the world . . .
When a lamp is lit,
it is not put *under the meal-tub,**
but on the lamp-stand,
where it gives light to everyone in the house.'

(Matt. 5.14ff.)

---

*cp. Mark 4.21–23 adds 'or *under the bed?*' This conjures up a more amusing picture, perhaps too far-fetched for Matthew to include.

In the same way his disciples by their actions . . .

> 'must shed light among your fellows, so that, when they
> see the good you do, they may give praise to your Father
> in heaven.'

In his warning on swearing (Matt. 5.33ff.) Jesus, having
forbidden his hearers to swear at all, reminds them that they
cannot turn one hair of their head white or black.*

> 'Plain "Yes" or "No" is all you need to say.'

In today's world most people are greatly concerned about
money: for many it has become the major anxiety of their lives,
leading to greed, selfishness, crime, and all forms of mental
breakdown. Our Lord's words on anxiety are arranged by
Matthew to follow immediately after . . .

> 'You cannot serve God and Money.'**

The most satisfactory explanation of Matt. 6.25–34 for
Christians today is that, although in the modern world we have
to be able to pay our way, we should not concern ourselves too
much with unnecessary worries about material things.

Jesus underlines this lesson in his customary reference to
Nature by stating and asking some obvious truths.

> 'Is there a man of you
> who by anxious thought
> can add a foot to his height?'

That was in the days of sandals, not platform heels.

Again, Jesus asks a question which demands an obvious
'No!' when warning about false prophets . . .

---

*Dyeing is an ancient art mentioned several times in the OT but restricted to
garments, not hair.
**Note capital M in New English Bible – the twentieth century god.

BEFORE   AFTER

*Is there a man of you
who by anxious thought
can add a foot to his height?'*

'who come to you dressed up as sheep while underneath they are savage wolves.'

(Matt. 7.15)

What vivid imagery. The original 'wolf in sheep's clothing' long before Little Red Riding Hood's old grandmother!

False prophets, like wolves – and people generally – often hide themselves under a disguise, a pose, but their actions will reveal their true intentions.

'You will recognise them by the fruits they bear.'

(Matt. 7.16)

And then there comes the whimsical question which provided another mental picture to treasure.

'Can *grapes* be picked from *briars*,
or *figs* from *thistles*?'

Of course they can't! That's obvious!

'That is why I say
you will recognise them by their fruits.'

(Matt. 7.20)

We have already noticed how the Pharisees condemned Christ's way of life. Some of their lawyers showed their disgust on one occasion when he was found seated at table in Matthew's house, eating with tax-gatherers and other bad company. Jesus' reply was typically memorable and amusingly obvious.

'It is not the healthy that need a doctor, but the sick.'

(Mark 2.15–17)

Jesus encourages his followers to persevere in their prayers. In two parables Luke shows how persistence will be answered. The first 'situation comedy' concerns a neighbour who is awakened by a friend at midnight.

40

'Lend me three loaves, for a friend of mine on a journey
has turned up at my house, and I have nothing to offer
him.'

Very inconvenient, and you can imagine the sleepy, grumbling
reply of the man who has probably had to get out of his bed to
answer his friend's request.

> 'Do not bother me.
> The door is shut for the night;
> my children and I have gone to bed;
> and I cannot get up and give you what you want.'

But on second thoughts . . . if he doesn't meet the request his
midnight suppliant will continue knocking until the whole
household is woken up. Oh well, I'd better give the blighter
what he wants. The obvious solution. How much more is a
Loving Father likely to answer the prayers of his faithful people
(Luke 11.5–10)! A simple, but brilliant, little parable, and so
funny if you imagine the situation in detail.

The second 'situation comedy' is about a persistent widow
who makes life such a misery for a judge that he accedes to her
demands.

> '. . . this widow is so great a nuisance that I will see her
> righted before she wears me out with her persistence.'

How much more will God listen to the prayers of his chosen
and answer them (Luke 18.1–8)!

Continuing the theme of answer to prayer, both Matthew
and Luke record a typical set of questions obviously demand-
ing the answer 'No!'.

> 'Is there a man among you who will offer his son a *stone*
> when he asks for *bread*,
> or a *snake*
> when he asks for *fish*?'

> (Matt. 7.9ff.)

No, of course not!

> 'Is there a father among you who will offer his son a *snake*
> when he asks for *fish*,
> or a *scorpion*
> when he asks for an *egg*?'

(Luke 11.11ff.)

Likewise.

By asking questions which demand an obvious negative and draw an amusing picture at the same time, Jesus is able to compare the goodness of God and his willingness to answer our prayers.

> 'If you, then, bad as you are,
> know how to give your children what is good for them,
> how much more will your heavenly Father
> give good things to those who ask him!'*

The following parable, featured only in Luke, borders on the absurd, and demands another very obvious 'No!' And yet it carries a serious application. Again the amusing picture, simple, and straight from life. But is it likely that a master will say to his servant when he returns from ploughing or minding sheep, 'Come along at once and sit down'? No, of course he won't! Quite the opposite.

> 'Prepare my supper,
> fasten your belt,
> and then wait on me while I have my meal;
> you can have yours afterwards.'

Jesus makes the implication more obviously.

> 'Is he grateful to the servant
> for carrying out his orders?'

No, indeed. It is his duty. And so it is the duty of the servants of God to follow his Will, expecting nothing in return (Luke 17.7–11). St Ignatius' inspired prayer sums this up . . .

> Teach us, good Lord,
> To serve thee as thou deservest:
> To give and not to count the cost;
> To fight and not to heed the wounds;
> To toil and not to seek for rest;
> To labour and not to ask for any reward
> Save that of knowing that we do thy Will.

There is no merit table in the Kingdom of God. Strict adherence to the Law brought no bonus points.

*In the NEB Luke defines 'good things' as the Holy Spirit.

Chapter 7

Riddles and playing on words

ONE OF the most familiar riddles in the Bible is the one Samson asks in the Book of Judges (14.1–20), which leads to unhappy consequences. Samson is on his way down to Timnath to see his Philistine girl-friend when he is attacked by a lion. 'The spirit of the Lord suddenly seized him and, having no weapon in his hand, he tore the lion in pieces as if it were a kid.'

The next time Samson visited his betrothed 'he turned aside to look at the carcass of the lion, and he saw a swarm of bees in it, and honey.'

Later at the wedding feast Samson asks his bride's guests to answer his riddle –

> 'Out of the eater came something to eat; out of the strong came something sweet.'

The bride's family fail to come up with the answer, so they persuade her to coax the solution out of her husband.

> 'What is sweeter than honey?
> What is stronger than a lion?'

When he realises that he has been tricked by his spouse Samson is understandably furious.

> 'If you had not ploughed with my heifer, you would not have found out my riddle.'

Hardly an endearment on their wedding-night. Samson returns home enraged, and his erstwhile spouse transfers her affections to his best-man. Who says that only the twentieth century is liberated!

A riddle is a question or statement designed to test the ingenuity or understanding of the listener.

There are two particularly clear riddles in the Gospels. Jesus probably asked many more, but, although remembered, they have not found a place in the Gospel narratives. These two examples demonstrate the subtlety of Christ's wit. He certainly gave his opponents something to puzzle over.

Following the cleansing of the Temple Jesus is later asked by the chief priests, lawyers, and elders, from whom does Jesus receive his authority for acting in such a manner (Mark 11.27ff.).

Jesus parries their question by asking them one: if they can answer his, then he will answer theirs!

> 'The baptism of John: was it from God, or from men?
> Answer me.'

This was a highly-charged riddle. Their answer would reveal whether they acknowledged John the Baptist's divine mission, or not. Neither answer was satisfactory. They knew they were snookered and refuse to commit themselves. Did Jesus, perhaps, smile when he replied,

> 'Then neither will I tell you
> by what authority I act.'

In his final week in Jerusalem our Lord was asked questions by his opponents in an attempt to trap him, to get him to say something that could be used as evidence against him.

The Synoptics record four particular incidents: Christ's authority, paying tribute to Caesar, resurrection of the dead, and the chief commandment (Mark 12.13ff.). There were probably many more – comparable to the indiscriminate hounding of people in the news by the modern Press. Finally, Mark, with the right sense of literary timing, places a question from Jesus (to the Pharisees in Matt. 22.41–46) in the form of a riddle.

'David himself said, when inspired by the Holy Spirit,
"The Lord said to my Lord,
'Sit at my right hand until I make your enemies your
footstool.'"
David himself calls him "Lord";
how can he also be David's son?'

(Mark 12.35–37; Luke 20.41–44)

Jesus, assuming that it was David who wrote Psalm 110,
quotes the first verse, understood by the theologians of the first
century to refer to the Messiah, the Lord's Anointed, the
Deliverer of Israel, for whose coming the Jewish nation longed.
Hence the conundrum. If David calls him 'Lord', how can the
Messiah be referred to as the Son of David?

Not perhaps a relevant question for us today, but clearly a
riddle which caused Christ's opponents a great deal of thought.
Jesus with disarming wit gives the Pharisees a catch-question to
puzzle over. And no doubt causes a little amusement for his
listeners who enjoy seeing the legalistic Pharisees on the receiv-
ing end for a change.

Playing on words

There are at least three examples of Jesus 'playing on words' in
the Gospels, maybe more. Apart from situation comedy, much
of today's humour is based on word-play. Examples are
infinite, ranging from the subtle to the outrageous.

The most obvious example from the Gospels comes at the
call of Christ's first disciples. Jesus is walking by the shore of
the Sea of Galilee when he sees Simon and his brother Andrew
on the lake at work with a casting-net; for they were *fishermen*.
Jesus said to them,

'Come with me,
and I will make you *fishers of men*.'

(Mark 1.16–20)

Peter isn't likely to forget that momentous experience,
although it is probable that they had already had some contact

'I will make you fishers of men.'

with Jesus (cf. John 1.35–42) and were awaiting Christ's call to follow at once.

When Jesus plays on the word *'leaven'* (Mark 8.14ff.) his disciples take him literally, and so he has to explain the pun to them. I hope Jesus wasn't as exasperated as Mark records. The first disciples aren't the only ones who haven't shared Christ's humour.

John in his intuitive portrayal of the life of Christ mentions at the end of one of Jesus' lengthy discourses what must be almost a sigh of relief,

> 'His disciples said,
> "Why this is plain speaking;
> this is no figure of speech . . ."'

(John 16.29)

Mark alone in his list of the Twelve (3.13–19) adds that the sons of Zebedee, James and his brother John, were given the name Boanerges, Sons of Thunder, by Jesus. Presumably what we call a nickname, either because they were twins, or, more probably, because they were quick-tempered (cf. Mark 9.38f; Luke 9.52ff.).

Christ had a nickname for Simon, too. Another example of his amusing word-play. This is preserved in Matthew's Gospel alone and follows the disciple's identification of Christ as

48

Messiah at Caesarea Philippi (Matt. 16.13–20). Jesus plays on the word *petros* (rock):

> 'You are *Peter*, the *Rock*;
> and on this *rock* I will build my church.'

Bearing in mind Christ's parable in Matthew 7.24–27 about the man 'who had the sense to build his house on rock, this seems a typical Christ remark, rather than a later addition to bolster up the supremacy of Rome!

Only Luke tells us of the visit of Jesus to the house of Martha and Mary (10.38–42). Martha, intent on being a good hostess while her sister 'entertains' their guest, becomes 'distracted by her many tasks' and, understandably, loses her cool. She rushes into the lounge, all het up, and momentarily lets fly at Jesus and her sister,

> 'Lord, do you not care that my sister has left me to get on with the work by myself? Tell her to come and lend a hand.'

Jesus endeavours to calm her down. There's no need to go to all this trouble for him. (Bread and cheese will do*). And then he probably smiled kindly at her and made a little joke (not obvious in NEB translation).

> 'The *part* that Mary had chosen is best; and it shall not be taken away from her.'**

I always feel sympathy for Martha. She was trying to put on such a good show for her guest, but she overdid it. Not an uncommon failing among hostesses. Real human situation this. And I expect Jesus made sure that it ended happily for her.

There are numerous examples from the Gospels of our Lord being outspoken. Luke records one particular occasion when He calls Herod Antipas 'that fox'.

---

*Inferred, in colloquial expression.
**The Greek word for 'part' also has the meaning 'portion' or 'helping' of food. Martha might have appreciated the word-play!

Some friendly Pharisees warn Jesus that Herod is out to kill him. His reply is vehement and challenging (Luke 13.31–33). In biblical terms the fox is a destructive animal, but in Greek and, consequently, in English, he becomes a symbol of cunning. However, the word in Rabbinic literature suggests a worthless and insignificant person, and Jesus may well have meant that Herod was a twit!

Chapter 8

Parables

ONCE UPON a time a man bought a parrot. 'Will the bird talk?' he asked the proprietor of the pet shop.

'Well, sir, to tell you the truth, he's a nervous fellow. Make him feel at home first and he'll soon start.' So the man bought a little mirror to go in the parrot's spacious new cage. A few days passed. Not a word. The parrot's new owner returned, disappointed, to the pet shop.

'Give him one of these little swings,' suggested the shopkeeper. 'He'll love it.'

Two days later the parrot's owner, dissatisfied, called again at the pet shop. This time he was persuaded to buy a seesaw.

'That'll encourage him,' the proprietor said. 'You won't be able to stop him talking.'

A few days passed. Then once more the parrot's owner, distraught, burst into the pet shop. 'He's dead!'

The proprietor commiserated. 'He didn't by chance say anything before he passed away?' he asked kindly.

'As a matter of fact he did,' replied the bereaved owner. 'He gasped out, "Do they sell bird seed at that shop?"'

The simple moral to be drawn from this pathetic tale is that we often overlook, or are oblivious of, the basic essentials of life, physical and spiritual.

I remember a vicar once writing to me about a Confirmation candidate. 'He has everything money can buy – and nothing else.'

Picture stories

A parable* is simply a colourful illustration in story form from which the listener is encouraged to draw some conclusion. It is the elaboration of a figure of speech. We have already seen how Jesus in his teaching used pictorial metaphors and similes to appeal to his audience and to give them something to remember which they might think about afterwards. Instead of using academic terms to convey the Truth Jesus regularly used 'picture stories'.

When asked 'Who is my neighbour?' Christ didn't answer in sociological language talking about 'community' and 'interdependence'. He told the story of the Good Samaritan, lampooning the priest and Levite, and commending with subtle irony the kindness of the much-despised Samaritan (Luke 10.25–37).

Each parable story is a characterisation or caricature which can be observed in everyday life, drawn either from Nature, e.g. the Sower, mustard seed, tares, etc., or from Christ's appreciation of his fellow beings, e.g. the labourers in the vineyard, lost coin, importunate friend, etc.

Parables were a recognised mode of teaching long before Jesus told them so brilliantly (cf. Judges 9.7–15; 2 Samuel 12.1–7). He was without doubt an expert in the art of story-telling. Although some have probably been misquoted and embellished, we may be confident that here is the bulk of our Lord's authentic teaching.**

It is evident from Mark 4.14–20 – the 'interpretation' of the Parable of the Sower – that the parables were often seen as allegories (in which each detail is of identifiable significance) by the Early Church, and this misunderstanding has led to a lot of unnecessary difficulties, and also to the loss of some of our Lord's humour.***

---

*masal (Hebrew) – mathla (Aramaic) covers a wide area of meaning. In the New Testament a parable if essentially a 'picture story' making one particular point.

**'We stand right before Jesus when reading his parables' – J. Jeremias *The Parables of Jesus*, SCM Press. A 'must' for any study of the parables.

***The serious Parable of the Wicked Husbandmen – Mark 12.1–9 – is intended by Jesus to be taken as an allegory.

Christ's stories stimulate the hearer into thought and action. Likewise, readers of the Gospels today are challenged to draw their own conclusion from each parable and to act, applying the lesson taught to their own lives. Each one should be read carefully and thoughtfully. All will instruct, encourage, and sometimes tease. All demand some sort of response.

Above all, parables paint an unforgettable picture. We must visualise each one in our own mind, at the same time, if possible, aware of the context in which Jesus first told it.

One thing is clear. Jesus did not use parables to flummox people. That was not his purpose at all. Most leading scholars are agreed that the explanation given in Mark 4.10–12 (Matt. 13.10–15, Luke 8.9,10) is mistaken along with the interpretation that follows. It just wasn't Christ's way – nor his style.

He explains the Kingdom of God to his close followers because it is soon going to be their responsibility to carry on his mission:

> 'The Kingdom of God is upon you;
> Repent, and believe the Gospel.'
>
> (Mark 1.15)

But he has to tell parables to the general public because, as Isaiah also realised, they are totally lacking in spiritual insight. A rueful, but compassionate reference.

> 'You may hear and hear,
> but you will never understand;
> you may look and look,
> but you will never see.
> For this people's mind has become gross;
> their ears are dulled,
> and their eyes are closed . . .'
>
> (Matt. 13.14,15; Isaiah 6.9,10)

It would have been a waste of time talking to people about the Kingdom of God in metaphysical language. Our Lord was not a greek philosopher; not the founder of one of the numerous mystery religions or Gnostic sects which proliferated

53

'How hard it is for a rich man to enter the Kingdom of Heaven.'

throughout the Greek-speaking world. And so in his parables he describes what the Kingdom of God is *like* and how people should face up to this crisis. Yes, crisis, e.g. the faithful and unfaithful servants, the ten bridesmaids, the great feast, the talents, etc. Not just a story with a simple meaning: for those with eyes to see – the perception – a personal spiritual challenge. The time for decision.

Not only is this demanded or implied in the parables of the Kingdom. In all Christ's parables (e.g. Good Samaritan, unforgiving servant, prodigal son, etc.) there is that underlying challenge to all of us. Discipleship in the Kingdom of God calls for a radical re-think of our own position. 'Fresh skins for new wine'.

Much has been written about the parables, and those fascinated by their form and content will have read C. H. Dodd's *The Parables of the Kingdom* and Joachim Jeremias' *The Parables of Jesus*. It is sufficient here to suggest the various places where Christ's sense of humour may be glimpsed.

Vivid picture

In the parable of the sower Jesus draws a vivid picture of the various factors which can threaten and destroy the seed, but the sower knows that despite all this there will be an abundant harvest in the end. Perhaps to emphasise this cheerful encouragement Jesus' claim of 'a hundredfold' is a trifle exaggerated, at least in the agricultural sphere. What Christ is saying to his disciples is this, 'Don't be discouraged at the opposition; God's will triumphs in the end.' (Mark 4.1–9; cf. 4.26–29)

The introduction into the parable of the tares of 'an enemy' may have added a subtle twist, but there is some probability that this may be the invention of the Evangelist. The explanation seems to be. It is not an allegory, but an insistence to let God act in his own way in his own time.

Forgiveness is an essential quality required of all members of the Kingdom of God. Christ emphasises this on several occasions, notably in the parables of the prodigal son and the unmerciful servant (cp. Luke 7.37–50).

In the latter story (Matt. 18.23–35) Jesus contrasts the colossal debt owed by the first servant to the king ('ran into millions') with the paltry amount owed by a fellow-servant ('a few pounds'). There are other surprising details in the story which make it all the more memorable: the sale of the wife (forbidden by Jewish law) and the use of torture (a heathen punishment). The point of the parable is clear (cf. Matt. 6.14,15).

> 'How blest are those who show mercy; mercy shall be shown to them.'
>
> (Matt. 5.7)

The mercy of God is again illustrated in the parable of the labourers in the vineyard (Matt. 20.1–16). Jesus probably was amused at the indignant response of his listeners at what on first sight seems an unfair decision. Enough to make a Trade Unionist have a sleepless night. Why should the latecomers receive the same wage as those who had sweated throughout the day? This is taking social welfare too far!

This is a story which Jesus may have told with tongue in cheek. A little puzzle to ponder over. Apply it to God's Kingdom. God's mercy is for all men and women. For those, like the elder son in Luke 15.25–32 and the Pharisees, God's mercy is the same, no more, no less, as his mercy for the sinners who repent at the last moment.

When reading the parable of the great supper I have always felt that the apologies given by the invited guests are pretty poor excuses, especially by the man recently married. Why didn't he ask if he could bring his wife as well; surely everyone would like to meet her? This, of course, is to miss the point – as well as introducing a red-herring. The first two apologise that they will be a little late because they have some business to attend to at the end of the day – we call it 'working late at the office' nowadays. It is only the third man who says definitely, 'I cannot some.'

Jesus in this story shows that these three characters have missed their opportunity, and others will be invited to take their places (Luke 14.15–24; cp. Matt. 22.1–14). How brilliantly our Lord pictures the self-righteous Pharisees who have rejected Jesus' invitation to enter the Kingdom of God and the Gentiles 'on the highways and along the hedgerows' who respond to Christ's preaching.

It is interesting to note the divergencies in the accounts of Matthew and Luke. This gives a good illustration of how Christ's parables were developed by the Evangelists; how the simple story was allegorised and theologised by well-meaning preachers and teachers, and the point missed or altered to suit the contemporary scene.

The parable of the ten virgins – the NEB calls them plainly, and more appropriately, girls (better still, bridesmaids) – verges on situation comedy. There's a lesson to be learnt from it, nonetheless. One quintet is prepared, the other not. When the bridegroom arrives there is the crisis: five are ready for it, five not. Jesus has come: some are ready for him, some not. It's as simple as that. The rest is vivid description which was later allegorised and the humour lost (Matt. 25.1–13).

Luke 13.25ff. also includes the 'knock, knock, open the door' ending, and it seems likely that the two parables have the same common source.

Is it reading too much into Christ's subtle wit to note that oil is a symbol of repentance, and that the girls who were ready had some and the others did not?

Two other parables describe in effective scenes the necessity of being ready to receive the lord and master – the faithful and unfaithful servants and the vigilant servants. Both are told with a certain anticipatory relish, and shafts of gentle humour lighten up the night as we, too, wait . . . and wait until we realise that the crisis is upon us. What an unpleasant picture of the unfaithful servant Jesus portrays! He deserves his place with the hypocrites,

> 'where there is wailing and grinding of teeth'.

What spine-chilling imagery (Matt. 24.45–51; Luke 12.42–46; cp. Mark 13.33–37).

An unlikely reversal of roles occurs for the faithful servants in Luke 12.35–38, and yet it all agrees with our Lord's teaching on his own position –

> 'For who is greater –
> the one who sits at table
> or the servant who waits on him?
> Surely the one who sits at table.
> Yet here am I among you like a servant.'
>
> (Luke 22.27)

Spiritual capital

The parable of the talents in Matthew 25.14–30 and the parable of the pounds in Luke 19.12–27 must be variants of the same story. Editorial additions have probably been made to both and their final interpretations influenced by the primitive Church. However, there are grounds for seeing in what must have been the original story a caricature (or 'send up') by Jesus of the Old Testament idea of God as Judge. The revelation of God has been entrusted, like the talents or the pounds, to various people. Some – like the disciples – have already shed their light among their fellows (Matt. 5.14–16) and are fishing for men by sowing the seed (what splendid mixed metaphors!). They will increase God's revelation. But there are others – like the self-centred Jews, either Pharisees or priests – who have kept God's revelation to themselves, and have thereby lost it. These two parables are lessons in how to invest spiritual capital, and as such are very relevant to the Church today.

One of the channels of God's revelation is through acts of kindness, and this is given adequate expression in Matthew's parable of the Last Judgement (Matt. 25.31–46). Jesus borrows from Daniel 7.13–15 and Ezekiel 34.17, using apocalyptic language, to set the scene for his thought-provoking dialogue. And there is, perhaps, a slight touch of humour even in this. The sheep on the king's right hand are somewhat perplexed when he says,

> '. . . For when I was hungry,
> you gave me food;
> when thirsty,
> you gave me drink;
> when I was a stranger
> you took me into your home,
> when naked
> you clothed me;
> when I was ill
> you came to my help,
> when in prison
> you visited me.'

The 'sheep' reply,

> 'Lord, when was it that we saw you hungry
> and fed you,

or thirsty
and gave you drink,
a stranger
and took you home,
or naked
and clothed you?
When did we see you ill
or in prison,
and come to visit you?'

The king answers,

'I tell you this:
anything you did for one of my brothers here,
however humble,
you did for me.'

Acts of kindness are the expected manifestation of belief in
God. What is revolutionary in the above parable is this:
showing kindness to others is showing kindness to Christ
himself (cf. Hebrews 13.1–3).

Yet another superb story is the parable of the prodigal son in
which Jesus shows his critics God's concern for the lost; the
sinners and tax-gatherers. No wonder this exquisite portrayal
of 'the rake's progress' is one of the best known of biblical
stories (Luke 15.11ff.).

The NEB translation adds colloquial expression to the
picture – 'turned the whole of his share into cash', 'reckless
living', 'he began to feel the pinch'. You can see it all, including
his degradation amongst the pigs. True to life, repentance soon
follows, and the sinner returns home. What a surprise awaits
him. His father is overjoyed to welcome him back – not his
elder brother. Like the Pharisees he took offence. No mercy, no
forgiveness, no love. But the father invites him, too, to join in
the celebrations. The Good News is for all, but some will not
accept it.

Most commentators admit that the parable of the unjust
steward (Luke 16.1–13) is rather puzzling. The story is

straightforward – although in essence somewhat crooked – to the end of verse 7. Now comes the difficulty in v.8:

> 'The master applauded the dishonest steward for acting so astutely . . .'

The NEB without hesitation attributes this highly surprising commendation to the master who has been cheated. Some scholars suggest that 'the master' may refer to 'the Master' – and this makes it all the more puzzling. Unless Jesus, in either case, is joking. Or maybe it is no laughing matter. It is not a commendation of dishonesty, but immediate and astute action in the face of a crisis. And we have already seen how Jesus saw his mission in terms of a crisis.

Verse 8b suggests that men of the world are more astute at their worldly business than the 'otherworldly' are at theirs; the latter should take every opportunity to advance their 'other-worldly' business.

It seems probable that vv.9–13 are additional comments, possibly of our Lord's, but collected by Luke under the subject-heading of 'mammon'. All exhibit worldly wisdom leading towards 'otherworldliness'. The generous use of riches is a sensible preparation for the future.

Jesus illustrates the insecurity of wealth, in which so many modern-day people trust, with his light-hearted parable of the rich fool who pulls down his store-houses to build larger ones for his heavy yield. Then he will sit back and enjoy himself in real Epicurean style.

> 'Man, you have plenty of good things laid by, enough for many years:
> take life easy,
> *eat, drink, and enjoy yourself.*'

Jesus throws in the well-known Epicurean maxim to add some philosophical colour to the man's selfish deliberations.

> 'But God said to him, "You fool,
> this very night you must surrender your life;

you have made your money –
who will get it now?"'

(Luke 12.16–21)

What a vivid story to remember. The comic futility of man's efforts without respect for the Will of God. What insight Jesus had into human folly.

The rich man/poor man theme is given a clever twist by Jesus in the Dives and Lazarus story. Our Lord caricatures the prosperous and self-indulgent Sadducee, unworried by belief in an after-life and determined to enjoy the present, in complete contrast to the poverty and suffering of Lazarus. In scene two the roles are reversed. In contemporary Jewish imagery Jesus pictures Dives in Hades, Lazarus in 'Heaven'. The ex-gourmet implores Father Abraham to send Lazarus to comfort him. No chance. There is 'a great chasm fixed' between them. Again Dives implores Abraham to send Lazarus, this time to warn his five brothers. No chance.

'They have Moses and the prophets;
let them listen to them,' says Abraham.

Dives is desperate. Surely if someone from the dead visits them they will repent? The final irony. Abraham refuses.

'If they do not listen to Moses and the prophets they will
pay no heed even if someone should rise from the dead.'
(Luke 16.19–31)

A final punch-line laden with significance. Many parables are not particularly light-hearted, but most contain flashes of subtlety, or irony, or graphic imagery. All add up to the composite picture of the Personality of our Lord.

Chapter 9

Throwaway lines and catch phrases

SOMETIMES it is the rueful comment at the end of a statement that supplies a touch of dry wit to Christ's teaching. Although some scholars would have us believe that this final line is an addition by either the Evangelist or by the Early Church.

In the Sermon on the Mount Jesus instructs his hearers to love not only their neighbour, but also their enemies.

> 'If you love those who love you,
> what reward can you expect?
> Surely the tax-gatherers do as much as that!'
>
> (Matt. 5.43ff.)

Remember that Jesus chose a tax-gatherer to be one of his disciples, and it is likely that Matthew compiled the Sermon. Did Jesus give Matthew a smile or a wink when he said that? Playful irony?

Jesus often warns against ostentation. In the Sermon he describes how the hypocrites show off in charity giving and prayer (Matt. 6.1–6).

> 'I tell you this:
> they have their reward already.'

Yes, people who show off tend to be seen – that's what they want, and that's their reward! And yet, like the Pharisees, they are not aware of the real impression they make on the passers-by.

Likewise, those who wish to convince others of their religious and ascetic fervour (Matt. 6.16–18)

> 'They make their faces unsightly
> so that other people may see that they are fasting.'

Jesus adds, with a smile perhaps, his well-remembered rueful comment,

> 'I tell you this:
> they have their reward already.'

They certainly succeed in looking miserable! What a contrast to the good cheer of Christ's Gospel. It should be a time for rejoicing – 'The Kingdom of God is at hand.'

Perhaps Matt. 6.34, although not amusing, should be classed as a throwaway line. Jesus has been encouraging his listeners not to be anxious about the future. There is enough evil in the present without looking forward to the future.

> 'Each day has troubles enough of its own.'

When contrasting his public image with that of John the Baptist, Jesus, acknowledging that it is impossible to please everyone, adds,

> 'And yet God's wisdom is proved right by its results.'
> (Matt. 11.19)

In his treatment of the new wine and old wineskins parable Luke adds what may be a rueful comment of our Lord (omitted from some texts) on the generally conservative attitude towards change. He has already shown his listeners that his new teaching cannot be fitted into Judaism. The old must be completely replaced – fresh skins for new wine (Matt. 9.16,17; Mark 2.21,22; Luke 5.36–38)! His opponents don't want change. And his listeners probably don't either!

Jesus adds ruefully? whimsically? teasingly?

'And no one after drinking old wine wants new; for he says, "The old wine is good."'

'And no one after drinking old wine wants new; for he says, "The old wine is good."'

(Luke 5.39)

Jesus is well aware of people's dislike or fear of change.
Other throwaway lines, not necessarily humorous, include:

'Wherever the corpse is,
there the vultures will gather.'

(Matt. 24.28; Luke 17.37)

'For if these things are done when the wood is green,
what will happen when it is dry?'

(Luke 23.31)

'Foxes have their holes,
the birds their roosts;
but the Son of Man has nowhere to lay his head.'

(Matt. 8.20)

In the third example Jesus may be referring to Herod and his followers when he uses the word 'foxes' (cf. Luke 13.32) and to the Gentiles as 'birds' (cf. Mark 4.30–32).

Catch phrases
Catch phrases are not limited to the TV screen –

> 'Didn't he do well!'
> 'Who loves you, baby?'
> 'I didn't get where I am today . . .'
> 'Nice one, Cyril.'

A few of Christ's catchy expressions remain for us in the pages of the Gospels. Often when in confrontation with the Pharisees or lawyers Jesus refers them to the Scriptures on which they were the acknowledged experts, teasingly suggesting,

> 'Have you never read the text . . .?'
> or 'Can it be you have never read . . .?'
> > (Matt. 12.13; 19.4; 21.16,42; 22.31;
> > Mark 2.25; 12.10,24; Luke 6.3)

A tinge of sarcasm perhaps? More like cheerful banter intended to embarrass, not hurt.

Another catch phrase which is likely to have been remembered, based on Deuteronomy 29.4 and Ezekiel 12.2, appears in two or three incidents, notably at the end of the parable of the sower.

> 'If you have ears (to hear – Mark, Luke), then hear.'
> (Matt. 11.15; 13.9,43; Mark 4.9,23; Luke 8.8; 14.35)

Ears of corn are not mentioned in the Sower parable, so it is wishful thinking to see a play on words here!

Peter's concern for some future reward (Matt. 19.30, Mark 10.31) – and who can blame him? – was answered, not unkindly, by Christ who warned that status and position in this world count for nothing.

One of many Christian paradoxes.

> 'Many who are first will be last,
> and the last first.'
>
> (Matt. 19.30; 20.16; Mark 10.31)

Mark applies this catch phrase at the incident when the disciples were arguing amongst themselves who was the greatest. Jesus sets a child in their midst, and puts his arm around the child:

> 'If anyone wants to be first,
> he must make himself last of all
> and servant of all.'
>
> (Mark 9.35)

There was, of course, the famous occasion at the Last Supper when Jesus himself acted out this paradox (John 13.1–17).

Luke enlarges the saying and loses much of its effectiveness, although he applies it more clearly to the day of judgement.

> 'Yes, and some who are now last will be first, and some who are first will be last.'
>
> (Luke 13.30)

The words of the Magnificat (Luke 1.51–53) are given full expression in another of Christ's well-known paradoxes. Jesus is warning his hearers – as usual – about the hypocrisy and ostentation of the doctors of the Law and the Pharisees.

> 'For whoever exalts himself will be humbled; and whoever humbles himself will be exalted.'
>
> (Matt. 23.12)

Luke records this catch phrase, appropriately, at the end of Christ's amusing parable of the place of honour at a wedding feast (Luke 14.6–11). What worldly wisdom! How well Jesus observed people. He knew how very important it was for some types to sit at the top table. What an embarrassing picture he draws of deflated pride – and rewarded humility. It's enough to make anyone chuckle, because it is such a delightful sketch of a particular type of person we meet today. No wonder Jesus found the Pharisees fair game.

Luke also places this catchy saying at the end of Christ's parable of the Pharisee and tax-gatherer at prayer, again constrasting the pride of the one with the humility of the other (Luke 18.9–14).

One of the characteristic sayings of the Fourth Gospel are the 'I am' passages:

> 'I am the bread of life' (6.35,41,48).
> 'I am the light of the world' (8.12)
> 'I am the door of the sheepfold' (10.7,9)
> 'I am the good shepherd' (10.11,14)
> 'I am the resurrection and I am life' (11.25)
> 'I am the way; I am the truth and I am life' (14.6)
> 'I am the real vine' (15.1,5)

A ready-made catch phrase first recorded in the burning bush incident (Exodus 3.14) and then at the publication of the Ten Commandments (Exodus 20.2). In both cases 'I am' represents the majesty and power of Almighty God. In the Fourth Gospel the expression introduces an allegory which reflects particular qualities and actions of Jesus recorded in the first three Gospels. It is probable, therefore, that it is a Johannine invention, but it may have been an authentic catch phrase opening to some of Christ's remarks.

Chapter 10

Having the last word

IT IS inevitable that Jesus should be seen to have the last word in conversation, and this is well demonstrated in the Temptations dialogue, however it is understood.

Our Lord's unforgotten punch lines end all argument: his actions emphasise his authority. Many examples can be cited – healing on the sabbath, the question of defilement, eating with sinners, forgiving sins, tax to Caesar, and that's just a few.

Before he healed Jairus' daughter Jesus unintentionally turned the mourners' wails into derisive laughter when he said,

'The child is not dead: she is asleep.'

Having turned out the disbelievers – still laughing? or howling again? – Jesus heals the twelve-year-old, and, according to Mark, adds the practical request that she should be given something to eat (Mark 5.35–43).

Luke includes the story of a woman who was leading an immoral life in the town who came to Jesus and received forgiveness. His host, a Pharisee, is understandably very shocked when she starts to kiss our Lord's feet. Jesus tells his host a parable which he then applies to the immediate situation.

'You see this woman?
I came to your house:
you provided no water for my feet;
but this woman has made my feet wet with her tears and wiped them with her hair.
You gave me no kiss;

69

but she has been kissing my feet ever since I came in.
You did not anoint my head with oil;
but she has anointed my feet with myrrh . . .'

(Luke 7.36–50)

It is unlikely that Jesus would have been so impolite as to take his host to task for his attitude unless he disguised his reproof in light-hearted irony or banter. We have our Lord's words in the Gospels, but not his tone of voice, nor do we see the kindly smile.

There may be some connection between the above incident and the story in John's Gospel, not found in most of the oldest and best manuscripts, and relegated in the NEB to the end of the Fourth Gospel, about Christ's sympathetic dealing with another adultress. Whatever the origin of this second incident, it exhibits Jesus in a playful mood until his serious conclusion. So typical.

The doctors of the Law and the Pharisees have evidently found the woman in a compromising position. She should be stoned. What is Christ's verdict? A test question. Jesus, feigning disinterest, bent down and wrote with his finger on the ground!

They continue to press their question. Jesus sits up – regards them with a look of innocent deliberation? – and gives a startling reply,

'That one of you who is faultless
shall throw the first stone.'

Then he bends down again and writes on the ground while his embarrassed questioners one by one fade away.

Left alone with the accused Jesus gives her a sympathetic rebuke.

'Nor do I condemn you.
You may go; do not sin again.'

(John 8.1–11)

Wherever this story comes from – and it could have come from the woman herself, perhaps – it expresses in action Christ's teaching on self-righteousness, personal judgement, and the necessity for divine forgiveness, and it reveals the characteristic humour and authority of Christ.

There is no room for sentimentality in commitment to Jesus. He makes this clear when a woman in the crowd, overcome with adoration, cries out,

> 'Happy the womb that carried you
> and the breasts that suckled you!'

(Luke 11.27)

'Blessed is thy mother' was a common Jewish greeting, but this outburst was going too far. Embarrassing.

Jesus retorts,

> 'No, happy are those who hear the word of God and keep it.'

(Luke 11.28)

Apart from the trials which led to the death of Christ on the Cross there is only one exchange in the Gospels (not Luke) in which Jesus appears to be outpointed – by a dogged Gentile mother.

If the accounts of Mark 7.24–30 and Matthew 15.21–29 are harmonised there is the following dialogue . . .

Woman   Sir! have pity on me, Son of David; my daughter is tormented by a devil.

(Disciples)   Send her away;
              see how she comes shouting after us.

Jesus   I was sent to the lost sheep of the house of Israel, and to them alone.

Woman   Help me, sir.

Jesus   Let the children be satisfied first: it is not fair to take the children's bread and throw it to the *dogs**

Woman   Sir, even the *dogs* under the table eat the children's scraps.

***

*'little dogs' is another, and kinder, translation.

'Even the dogs under the table eat the children's scraps.'

Jesus   For saying that, you may go home content: the unclean spirit has gone out of your daughter.

This conversation, far removed from our Lord's confrontations with the Pharisees, lawyers, and elders, at first sight seems to suggest that Jesus is treating the anguished Gentile mother with little respect and less sympathy. Not in character: can't be right. On the other hand, the woman's quick-witted reply wins Christ's admiration at once. 'I may be a dog,' she replies humbly, 'but even dogs get the scraps under the table which the children drop.'

It seems a possible solution to our Lord's apparent callousness to see in his remark a touch of ironic banter, a teasing comment on the traditional separatism of the Jewish nation from all other races: a misconception illustrated by the Book of Jonah and the parable of the good Samaritan. The tone of Christ's voice, the mildly sardonic fun-poking at Jewish prejudice, plus the twinkle in his eye, are missing from the Gospel record. After all, is it likely that Jesus would have been unkind to someone in trouble, whoever she was?

There is that marvellous conversation between Jesus and the Samaritan woman at the well recorded in chapter four of John's Gospel. However we understand his interpretative portrayal of Christ, it is clear that the writer presents an inspired revelation in this amusing dialogue. Here is Christ at once flippant and serious. It is a marvellous piece of writing.

Jesus	Give me a drink.
*Samantha**	What! You, a Jew, ask a drink of me, a Samaritan woman?
Jesus	If only you knew what God gives, and who it is that is asking you for a drink, you would have asked him and he would have given you living water.
Samantha	Sir, you have no bucket and the well is deep. How can you give me 'living water'? Are you greater than Jacob our ancestor, who gave us the well, and drank from it himself, he and his sons, and his cattle too?
Jesus	Everyone who drinks this water will be thirsty again, but whoever drinks the water that I shall give him will never suffer thirst any more. The water that I shall give him will be an inner spring always welling up for eternal life.
Samantha	Sir, give me that water, and then I shall not be thirsty, nor have to come all this way to draw.
Jesus	Go home, call your husband and come back.
Samantha	I have no husband
Jesus	You are right in saying that you have no husband, for, although you have had five husbands,

*Samaritan woman.

73

	the man with whom you are now living
	is not your husband;
	you told me the truth there!
Samantha	Sir, I can see that you are a prophet.

(John 4.7–19)

The conversation continues, and Jesus explains that the time has come,

> 'when those who are real worshippers
> will worship the Father in spirit and in truth.'

(John 4.23)

This leads on to one of the most inspired lines in the Fourth Gospel –

> 'God is spirit,
> and those who worship him
> must worship in spirit and in truth.'

(John 4.24)

However much John interprets the life of Christ, shafts of humour shine through to reveal the joyfulness of the Word made flesh.

Nowadays Beelzebub sounds a strange name – like one of the Wombles – but in New Testament times it was rather more serious. Baal zebul is translated 'Lord of the flies' or, in New Testament terms, 'Prince of devils'.

Jesus is accused by the doctors of the Law of black magic in his healing miracles, especially exorcism.

> 'He is possessed by Beelzebub'
> 'He drives out devils by the prince of devils'

(Mark 3.22ff.)

As usual Jesus has a simple, well reasoned answer for them, not without a humorous tone of banter.

> 'If a kingdom is divided against itself, that kingdom
> cannot stand;

if a household is divided against itself, that house will
never stand;
and if Satan is in rebellion against himself, he is divided
and cannot stand;
and that is the end of him.'

(Mark 3.25,26)

Note the repetitions, not so clear in Matthew's and Luke's
edited accounts, which make the argument easy to commit to
memory. Typical Jesus teaching pattern. He is saying in other
words – Satan isn't likely to cast himself out!

Matthew and Luke and Christ's challenge –

'If it is by Beelzebub that I cast out devils, by whom do
your own people drive them out?'

(Matt. 12.22–30; Luke 11.14–20)

Already, according to Mark 3.21, Jesus' family were anxious
about the power which he exhibited. Some people thought he
was 'out of his mind', and any form of madness was attributed
to Satanic possession. Our Lord's calm reasoning above makes
it certain that he was the sanest of all. It is probable that Jesus,
because of his attitude, was accused of being mad on a number
of occasions (cf. John 8.48ff.; 10.19,20). So was John the
Baptist. And Christians ever since.

If Beelzebub, using an alternative meaning, is translated
'Lord of the house', this provides a connecting-link as a
play-on-words leading into the short parable about the strong
man (i.e. Satan) in his house (Mark 3.27), extended more
colourfully by Luke 11.21,22, who is tied up and has his house
ransacked.

Jesus warns his followers on a number of occasions that they
will share his rejection and ridicule.

'If the master has been called Beelzebub, how much
more his household!'

(Matt. 10.25b)

A witty, though rueful, comment.

However, there are certain aspects of his mission about which Jesus refuses to jest. He is particularly conscious of the Power he has received from God, the manifestation of the Holy Spirit. Therefore to accuse Jesus of having an unclean spirit is unforgivable.

> 'Whoever slanders the Holy Spirit can never be forgiven.'
>
> (Mark 4.29)

There were times when Jesus was serious, very serious, and, no doubt, his listeners recognised it.

Chapter 11

Jesus and his disciples

EVEN CHRIST'S closest followers often took him seriously when they failed to see a joke or a piece of light relief. And sometimes Jesus teased them a little. He may have had nicknames for them all. It was not until after the Resurrection that Peter, the Rock, lived up to his name, but James and John, the Sons of Thunder, were particularly fiery (Luke 9.54).

The disciples must have enjoyed sharing Jesus' life-style at the start of his mission.

> 'Can you expect the bridegroom's friends to fast
> while the bridegroom is with them?'
>
> (Mark 2.19)

They 'broke' the Sabbath laws (Mark 2.23–28) and the ridiculously intricate ritual of purification (Mark 7). At first theirs was a happy-go-lucky existence given motivation and purpose by the dynamic message of the Kingdom of God. It was a joyful, exciting experience.

They sometimes found our Lord's parables a trifle hard to understand (Mark 4.10), but in private he explained it all to them. These men were the chosen few to broadcast his message to the world. Jesus sent them out in pairs and instructed them to take nothing for their journey except a stick: no bread, no pack, and no money (Mark 6.7ff.). Ideal, perhaps, in their circumstances, but not practicable for later missionaries. They must rely on hospitality. No time should be wasted on the unreceptive. They must 'shake the dust off their feet' as a warning to them. What a devastating expression, and at the same time an amusing picture to imagine. Jesus must have

77

known what it is like to have the front door slammed in his face. Parish visitors will appreciate this. There has to be some response to total rejection, and shaking the dust is far more subtle than shaking the fist at the discourteous householder as he returns grumpily to his telly. And more Christian, too (cp. Luke 10.10–12).

The feeding of the 5000/4000 was a remarkable event recorded, in all, six times in the four Gospels. John's account, maybe, reveals a humorous touch.

The disciples are anxious –

Jesus   'This is a lonely place, and the day has gone; send
           the people off to the villages to buy food.' There is
           no need for them to go; give them something to eat
           yourselves.

                                              (Matt. 14.15ff.)

Disciples All we have is five loaves and two fishes, nothing
           more –
           unless perhaps we ourselves are to go and buy
           provisions for all this company.

                                              (Luke 9.12ff.)

In Mark's two versions the disciples sound positively alarmed,

           'Are we to go and spend twenty pounds on bread to give
           them a meal?'

                                              (Mark 6.37)

           'How can anyone provide all these people with bread in
           this lonely place?'

                                              (Mark 8.4; cf. Matt. 15.33)

The words of the incident may vary but the gist of it is clear. However, in the version of the story in the Fourth Gospel it is Jesus who asks Philip,

           'Where are we to buy bread
           to feed these people?'

                                              (John 6.5ff.)

And then the Evangelist adds,

> 'This he said to test him;
> Jesus himself knew what he meant to do.'

Was our Lord gently teasing Philip who was getting het up? Isn't there an unmistakable pretended ignorance in that question? At this stage in his Gospel John is running parallel with the Synoptics, and it would be convenient if his account could be considered to be the basis of the others!

John leads on (6.22–58) to suggest what the other three Gospels imply that here is a proto-type Eucharist – a giving of thanks, a time of joyful fellowship, a spiritual breakthrough.

At times Jesus appears to show signs of irritation when his disciples are rather slow to understand. They didn't get his allusion to 'leaven'.

> 'Do you not understand even yet?
> How can you fail to see
> that I was not talking about bread?'
>
> (Matt. 16.5–12)

Mark's version – closer to the original – is even stronger.

> 'Have you no inkling yet?
> Do you still not understand?
> Are your minds closed?
> You have eyes: can you not see?
> You have ears: can you not hear?'
>
> (Mark 8.14–21)

The disciples were slow to appreciate Jesus' teaching on defilement (Mark 7.17ff.), and, perhaps understandably, they failed to grasp Christ's predictions of his Passion (Mark 9.32; Luke 9.45; 18.34). John suggests that they failed to see the significance of Christ's triumphal entry into Jerusalem (John 12.12–16).

The classic misunderstanding was Peter's at Caesarea Philippi. Having identified Christ as Messiah he reveals that his rock-like devotion is misguided. When Jesus speaks of his Passion Peter at once rebukes him: this is not the sort of Messiah Peter wants!

Jesus replies in that oft-quoted dismissal –

> 'Away with you, Satan;
> (you are a stumbling-block to me)*
> you think as men think,
> not as God thinks.'
>
> (Mark 8.33–35; Matt. 16.21–23)

In our attempt to appreciate the character of our Lord we tend to rely for our mental picture on *what* he said, not *how* he may have said it. An outburst of exasperation at his followers' stupidity and lack of perception, or a gentle, kindly word of disapproval spoken with a smile? Every good teacher knows which is the more effective. We are all pretty thick at times, and we need sympathetic handling!

Perhaps Jesus made his disciples grin at their own short-comings? Even Peter may have appreciated the contrast between being the Rock one moment and Satan the next (Matt. 16.13–23)!

One of the charms of simple folk – in contrast to the arrogance of self-possessed 'intellectuals' – is their muddled thinking and failure to see the point. Admittedly, Christ's new teaching was revolutionary, but its essential message was straightforward and uncompromising. Jesus revealed the Truth plainly.

One aspect of the Kingdom of God was that possessions and position count for nothing. But the age-old twentieth century concern for status and reward is very much in the minds of the disciples.

'Who is the greatest?'

Luke poses this question for the second time within the setting of the Last Supper (Luke 22.24–27).

*Only in Matthew.

On this occasion he records a particularly dry comment of Christ's which even the disciples would have appreciated.

'In the world kings lord it over their subjects; and those in authority are called their country's "*Benefactors*"'.

Benefactors indeed? Herod the Great? Pontius Pilate? Roman Emperor? What a joke!

Jesus often commended the faith of others – the woman with a blood disorder (Matt. 9.22; Mark 5.34; Luke 8.48), blind Bartimaeus (Mark 10.52; cf. Matt. 9.29; Luke 18.42), the Roman centurion (Matt. 8.10; Luke 7.9), and one of the ten lepers, a foreigner (Luke 17.19), et alia – but he also appears to scold his disciples for their lack of faith.

However we may take the storm on the lake, our Lord's words to his terrified followers at first sight seem somewhat harsh and without feeling for their predicament.

'Why are you such cowards?
How little faith you have!'
(Matt. 8.26; cf. 14.31; Mark 4.10; Luke 8.25)

He points to their lack of faith after the crestfallen disciples have failed to heal an epileptic boy (Matt. 17.19,20; Mark 11.20–24; cf. Luke 17.5,6).

Although Jesus may have reproved his disciples for their failure, I cannot imagine him doing it is anything but a kindly, understanding, almost jocular way. Our Lord was well aware of the qualities of love before 1 Corinthians 13 was written. That's why he was never angry or impatient with his followers. He treated them with sympathy – and good humour. But he told them plainly what to expect.

Our Lord was conscious of the cross which lay before him. He was well aware of the difficulties and dangers which his faithful disciples would have to face. His loving concern for them is expressed with moving sensitivity by the writer of the Fourth Gospel in chapter 17.

Jesus required his disciples to commit themselves totally to his mission – to preach the Kingdom of God.

'Anyone who wishes to be a follower of mine must leave
self behind;
he must take up his cross,
and come with me.
Whoever cares for his own safety is lost;
but if a man will let himself be lost for my sake and for
the Gospel,
that man is safe.
'What does a man gain by winning the whole world
at the cost of his true self?
What can he give to buy that self back?'
(Mark 8.34–37; Matt. 16.24–28; Luke 9.23–27)

This was all too much for the rich young man who wanted to
win eternal life without parting with his great wealth (Mark
10.17–22).

This dedication to Christ's mission demanded the severing of
all personal relationships (Matt. 10.37; Luke 14.25ff.), but the
gain was enormous. Jesus with typical light-heartedness
teaches the unity of all Christian people.

'Whoever does the will of God
is my brother, my sister, my mother.'
(cf. Mark 3.31–35)

However, Jesus warns that this commitment should not be
undertaken without careful thought beforehand. Two short
parables give this advise very clearly. The first paints an
amusing picture of an unbusinesslike builder.

'Would any of you think of building a tower without
first sitting down and calculating the cost,
to see whether he could afford to finish it?'

You expect Jesus to end at that, but he adds a laugh to
emphasise the permanent commitment required.

'Otherwise, if he has laid the foundation
and then is not able to complete it,

all the onlookers will laugh at him.
"There is the man," they will say,
"who started to build and could not finish".'

(Luke 14.28–30)

How well Jesus knew people!

He used another descriptive aphorism to stress the total surrender to discipleship.

'No one who sets his hand to the plough
and then keeps looking back
is fit for the Kingdom of God.'

(Luke 9.62)

'Would any of you think of building a tower without first sitting down and calculating the cost?'

The second short parable – about a king calculating his chances against another in battle – in contrast to the first is essentially serious. This ably demonstrates how the same lesson can be taught using opposite modes of approach.

Jesus encourages his disciples with typical cheerfulness. He must have spoken words of encouragement to them on many occasions. You never get the best response from people by rebuking them and being miserable. It was his own enthusiasm, his exhilarating challenge, his sheer Personality which won their complete dedication to his mission. And they worshipped him because he had gained their affection, not merely their obedience.

> 'Are not sparrows two a penny?
> Yet without your Father's leave
> not one of them can fall to the ground.
> As for you, even the hairs of your head have all been counted.'

A superb, engaging metaphor to stress the loving care of God for his own. And the final, inspirational punch line,

> 'So have no fear;
> you are worth more than any number of sparrows.'
>
> (Matt. 10.29–31)

And Jesus knows far better than they do what trials lie ahead for them.

> 'Look, I send you out like sheep among wolves; be wary as serpents, innocent as doves.'
>
> (Matt. 10.16)

What memorable similes with that characteristic touch of Jesus' own brand of humour. No wonder they followed This Man: no wonder they remembered His words.

84

Chapter 12

The shadow of the Cross

IT BECAME clear to our Lord that his mission would lead to the cross. There were too many people against him. Mark records three predictions which Jesus made to prepare his disciples for the crisis which lay in the immediate future (Mark 8.31; 9.31; 10.32f.).

He probably warned them on numerous occasions, not necessarily in such detail. His disciples are bewildered and will not believe it. This is not the Jesus they knew. How can a man who has healed the sick and taught about the New Life in the Kingdom of God die on a cross?

> 'A stumbling-block to Jews
> and folly to Greeks.'
>
> (1 Cor. 1.24)

Jesus knew the penalty for treason, even if it was on a trumped-up charge: he was well aware of Roman justice. He knew the sly malice of his opponents and the steps the authorities at Jerusalem were prepared to take to guard their own vested interests. He set his face towards Jerusalem, ready for the crisis which he realised was awaiting him there.

The happier days in Galilee are behind him now, and the Gospel narrative becomes tense and grave as he enters the Final Week – despite Luke's attempt to stress the triumph of the Cross. Here before our eyes is the historic conflict between the loving purpose of God and the evil designs of man. God's Way *v.* man's way, highlighted within world history by the shadow of the Cross.

Christ's triumphant entry alarms his opponents. Matthew records how the chief priests and scribes take exception to the cry of –

'Hosanna to the Son of David!' Jesus, with characteristic 'dig' at their knowledge of the Scriptures, reminds them of Psalm 8.2 (Matt. 24.17–21). In Luke 19.39f. the Pharisees request Jesus to reprimand his disciples for their unrestrained adulation. Jesus replies, rather banteringly,

> 'I tell you, if my disciples keep silence the stones will shout aloud.'

There follows the explosive incident in the Temple when Jesus drives out those who bought and sold and the money-changers. Jesus accuses the chief priests of letting this 'house of prayer' become 'a robbers' cave' – a brilliantly apt metaphor which held the crowd spellbound (Mark 11.15–19). Naturally, Jesus is questioned about his authority, and he answers by asking the chief priests, lawyers, and elders a riddle! (see p. 46). He is irrepressible.

The parable of the wicked husbandmen appears in all three Synoptics (see Mark 12.1–12). Jesus did not normally allegorise his stories, but that is no reason to assume that this is a later parable dreamed up by the Evangelist or the Early Church. Christ makes it very plain to his enemies that he is well aware of their intentions.

> 'Then they began to look for a way to arrest him, for they saw that the parable was aimed at them.'

Our final glimpse of Jesus at his devastating best is when he is questioned about paying tax to Caesar. As darkness gathers around him, Jesus deals with this catch question from a number of Pharisees and men of Herod's party sent to trap him –

> 'Are we or are we not permitted to pay taxes to the Roman Emperor?'

Christ realised how crafty their question was: if he said, 'Yes, pay taxes to the Emperor', the crowd would reject him: if he said 'No', he could be accused of treason.

> 'Why are you trying to catch me out?
> Fetch me a silver coin,
> and let me look at it.'

In other words, Jesus calls for what we call a 'visual aid' to provide a clear solution.

Imagine the situation. The wily Pharisees and crafty Herodians, the silent, spellbound crowd, and Jesus, calmly in control, waiting while a coin is produced.

Then Jesus smiles, looks at the coin, pretending to study it, holds it up, and asks with feigned innocence,

> 'Whose head is this, and whose inscription?'
> 'Caesar's', they replied.

And Jesus replies in those unforgettable words,

> 'Pay Caesar what is due to Caesar,
> and pay God what is due to God.'

> (Mark 12.13ff.)

As the tax money bears the Emperor's head and name, it is therefore his, so it should be paid to him. But there is also a duty to God, obedience to him in all things.

The riddle about the 'Son of David' ends this section in the Markan framework (see page 47). The tone of the Gospels now changes dramatically. The shadow of the Cross falls on Jesus and his small band of loyal followers. His enemies are all around him. The crisis has arrived.

The sympathetic action of the woman who annoints Christ at bethany (Mark 14.3–9) momentarily holds back the enveloping darkness, and then Judas goes to the chief priests. Jesus eats the Last Supper with his disciples, a fellowship meal, emotional and historic. Everyone must have sensed the tension of this poignant farewell. There was bread and wine, but the customary laughter and good humour was absent. A fearful sadness gripped them.

In this section Luke records Christ's final instructions to the Twelve. Now with bitter irony he warns them to be prepared.

> 'It is different now;
> whoever has a purse had better take it with him,
> and his pack too;
> and if he has no sword,
> let him sell his cloak to buy one.'
>
> (Luke 22.35–38)

The disciples take Jesus' remark literally, and he replies,

> 'Enough, enough!'

Scholars suggest many ingenious interpretations of this inconsistent passage. Surely Jesus didn't mean his disciples to fight their way out? Perhaps this remark, laden with irony, is a final feeble attempt to raise a smile to encourage his faithful few.

In the Garden of Gethsemane our Lord faces the impending crisis alone. Even his three closest friends fall asleep; they cannot watch with their Master for one hour. As he prepares himself for the agony to come, Jesus is momentarily tempted to escape.

> 'Abba, Father,
> all things are possible to thee;
> take this cup away from me.
> Yet not what I will, but what thou wilt.'
>
> (Mark 14.36)

Judas arrives and a clumsy arrest is made. The disciples scatter. Jesus is taken to the High Priest's house and is later 'found guilty' of blasphemy.

Early in the morning Jesus is brought to Pilate through whom the chief priests wish to obtain the death sentence. Their plan is to change the charge from blasphemy to treason (cf.

Luke 23.2), and consequently the Roman governor asks Jesus, 'Are you the king of the Jews?'

Despite Pilate's uneasiness about Christ's innocence, it is only a matter of time before the sentence is passed. Our Lord's distress is further aggravated by the bestial mockery of the soldiers who dress him in purple, plait a crown of thorns, and place it on his head. Here is the King of the Jewish nation: 'Hail, King of the Jews!'

Typical Roman humour. Barbaric and inhumane. A grim contrast to the compassionate love of God.

> 'Father, forgive them;
> they do not know what they are doing.'
>
> (Luke 23.34)

The history of the Christian Church right down to the present day catalogues the sufferings of those who have followed their Lord to his Cross. The 'Suffering Servant' of Isaiah 53 lives on in the twentieth century.

As Jesus hung on the Cross the passers-by hurled abuse at him. He had failed them. He was not the Messiah after all. Where was his army? Where was the throne of David? And the chief priests and lawyers laughed amongst themselves.

> 'He saved others,
> but he cannot save himself.'
>
> (Mark 15.31)

Their hardness of heart and total insensitivity to suffering is a stark denial of Christ's command,

> 'Love your enemies
> and pray for your persecutors.'
>
> (Matt. 5.45)

And even those crucified with him taunted him. The soldiers who cast lots for his clothes also joined in.

Jesus, whose light-hearted joy revealed a new spiritual

dimension, a new way of life in the Kingdom of God, dies on the Cross, jeers and ridicule ringing in his ears.

Three days later his few loyal followers had a remarkable experience which convinced them that Jesus was alive. And this experience has been repeated throughout the Christian centuries. The *joy* of the Resurrection brings faith and hope to millions of Christians. This is the joy which Jesus himself revealed to mankind.

> 'Be of good cheer:
> the Kingdom of God is here.'

Index
of Bible References

APPENDIX

Appendix of Verse

by Avery Goodman

(All characters are fictitious)

LBW (or 'The Lord Bishop's Wicket')
The Village Cricket Match
Mother's Ruin
Harvest Decorations
'Stoke Gabriel!'
Christmas Eve Crisis

Appendix of Verse

LBW
(Or 'The Lord Bishop's Wicket')

by Avery Goodman

The Bishop defiantly stood at the crease
Regarding the field with a nonchalant ease.
The pale-faced young Curate, poor trembling soul,
Walked back to his mark and waited to bowl.
'Give him an easy one which he can cart,'
Said the captain, the Dean, with a generous heart.
The bowler ran up, but then seconds later,
He'd rapped the Diocesan hard on the gaiter.

'How's that?' yelled the Dean with a confident shout.
The Umpire, a Canon, said: 'Sir, you are out.'
His Lordship aghast cried: 'I say, that's not cricket.
I haven't been two minutes here at the wicket.
Your theology, sir, is not good at all —
A Bishop's not out off his very first ball.'
The Curate triumphant said: 'Oh what bad luck.
My Lord you appear to be out for a duck!'
The Bishop smiled sourly. 'I'm always forgiving,
But don't come to me to ask for a Living.'
And so amidst somewhat embarrassed applause
He returned to the Pav. and put on his plus-fours.

The Village cricket Match

by Avery Goodman

On Midsummer Eve in a village in Devon
The Villagers play a College Eleven.
The parish churchwardens draw up a team
For this annual event on the small village green.
The church bells are ringing: the players in white:
The cherry trees blossom — 'tis a beautiful sight.

Each local player a great welcome gets,
And soon they are limbering up in the nets.
When the cows have been milked the game can begin:
The crowd becomes tense and the players look grim.
It may not be Melbourne, or Trent Bridge, or Lord's,
But many's the story which History records.

This countryside tale about Farmer Smith
Is regarded by some as part of a myth.
The Council were laying some sewer pipes which
Ran in a trench cut right through the pitch.
The farmer was passing along with his cows
And stopped for a moment to have a short browse.

The old Vicar's warden, inspecting the wicket,
Sadly pronounced 'It ain't fit for cricket.'
'I'll make 'ee a pitch,' said Smith with a gleam,
'As long as 'ee let's us be in yer team.
I ain't very 'ot, an' me bowlin' ain't fast.
An' I won't care a dam' if 'ee puts us in last.'

The offer accepted Smith started from scratch
Preparing a pitch for the forthcoming match.
Some hefty Young Farmers cut down the long grass
And the lads from the Club made the crease look first class.

The W.I. made up fancies and pies
All covered with muslin to keep off the flies.

The College were fielding a team of some power
Including a batsman who'd played once with Gower
The Villagers' side could not be compared,
And the College scored 200 for 7 declared.
The Village replied with 50 for 9.
Then Smith was sent in to play out the time.

The farmer reluctantly took up his stance,
Surveying the scene with a hesitant glance.
The bowler ran up and then moments later
He's rapped the old farmer hard on the gaiter.
'How's that?' yelled the team with a confident shout.
The umpire immediately said, 'Yes, he's out!'

The farmer aghast remained at the crease.
The umpire was startled and looked ill at ease.
'Hout?' asked the farmer. 'I ain't 'it the ball.
You can't call us hout: that ain't fair at all.'
'You're out,' smiled the captain. 'We've all just appealed.'
'All right,' growled the farmer. 'Get hout o' me field!'

Mother's Ruin

*Avery Goodman reveals the facts behind a
Mothers' Union slimming course*

The Mothers' Union secretary
Was a buxom Mum called Mary.
She had a charming husband, Jim,
Who one day said she ought to slim.
'Good gracious!' Mary cried aghast
'I've just survived a Lenten fast.'

The Verger's hefty sister, Kate,
Was also rather overweight.
The Rector's wife, whose name was Joan,
Tipped the scales at sixteen stone.
Said the Hon. Sec. with remorse:
'We'd better run a slimming course.'

They started eating Nimble bread
And gave up drinking tea in bed.
They cut out starchy foods and jam
And fancy cakes and fry and ham.
They only ate a little meat:
Gave up their lunch and had no sweets.

The Mothers' Union met and weighed
Twice a month, and bets were laid.
'I bet,' said the Enrolling Member,
Mary's slimmest by September.'
The Verger's sister, looking glum,
Said: 'Quote my odds at 10 to 1.'

Next day the Rector said to Jim:
'Your wife is looking pretty grim.'
Jim muttered: 'Well, I'm worried, Rector.

This slimming diet's nearly wrecked her.
The Rector said: 'We'll have to cure it.'
She's got this craze: I can't endure it.'

Next week when all the Mothers met
They thought the parish hall was let.
'A banquet's going on inside,'
Gasped Mary, peering starry-eyed.
'I've never seen so large a spread!'
'It's all for you,' the Rector said.

'Since you began this slimming game
The parish hasn't been the same.
You've lost your "go" and all your zeal.
It's time you had a decent meal.'
Said Mary: 'I've been such a clot.
Come on, girls, let's scoff the lot!'

Harvest Decorations

Avery Goodman

Some ladies in the church spend hours
Tidivating bowls of flowers.
They collar every silver vase,
And leave the rest with pots and jars.
The vicar will admire each one,
So no-one feels at all out-done.
And after every Harvest Festival
He tells his wife hers was the Best of All.

'Stoke, Gabriel!'

Avery Goodman

The Vicar was freezing,
The Curate was sneezing.
The church felt so terribly cold.
The choir with the shivers
Caught colds in their livers.
The system was ninety years old.

The PCC meeting
Complained of the heating.
They all said they froze in their pew.
The standing committee
Said that was a pity:
The boiler must have a new flue.

And while they debated
The system outdated
The Vicar arose from his chair.
'Let's hire a bloke who'll
Work down in the stoke-hole.
Let's stop all this talking hot air.'

Old Gabriel Davey,
Who'd been in the Navy,
Applied, and was given the post.
He told his employers
He'd worked in destroyers,
But liked stoking battleships most.

The Vicar looked drowsy,
The Curate felt lousy.
The temperature upward soon shot.
The small congregation

Was near suffocation.
The church was now rather too hot.

The verger perspiring,
The warmth not admiring,
Explained that the heat was too great.
'It's a church, not a boat.
We're on land, not afloat!'
The stoker replied 'Sorry, mate.'

This heart-warming story
Soon ended in glory,
For many folk made the itinerary.
They filled up the aisles,
Having journeyed for miles
To the best heated church in the deanery.

Christmas Eve Crisis

Avery Goodman

The Christmas tree fairy from high on her perch
Looked out through the window across to the church.
Up in the belfry the bells, loudly pealing,
Were filling the town with the Festival feeling.
The churchwarden stood with his back to the grate
Watching his sprightly young wife decorate.
'I think that my paperchains look rather jolly.'
'Yes,' he replied, 'but where's all our holly?'
'Oh, dear,' said his wife, 'I'm afraid I'm the culprit.
I used my last bit to cover the pulpit.'
'I don't think that's right,' the churchwarden said.
'You should have kept some for your own home instead.
In fact I think it's a very poor show.
All we've got now is that old mistletoe!'
The Christmas tree fairy continued to stare
Across to the church standing dark and austere.
The churchwarden followed her gaze and he sighed.
'It seems such a shame when there's plenty inside.
I'll take all this mistletoe over and swop it.'
'If the vicar finds out,' said his wife, 'then you'll cop it.'
He gave her a kiss: took his cap from its hook.
And walked to the church with a purposeful look.
The Christmas tree fairy looked on with suspicion,
Doubtful, it seemed, of the churchwarden's mission.
He soon reached the vestry, but to his dismay
He realised the vicar was not far away.
On a chair he observed the incumbent's old brolly
Protruding from under a large piece of holly.
The vicar appeared and said 'Care and share.
I say, have you got any mistletoe spare?'
The churchwarden smiled. 'Yes, sir. Take the lot,
Provided of course that you're willing to swop.'

The vicar agreed. The bargain was struck.
And each man went home amazed at his luck.
The Christmas tree fairy soon learned minutes later
The vicar had been on the very same caper.

Also published by The Canterbury Press Norwich:

Prayers for everyday use
CHRISTOPHER & JOSEPHINE BUNCH
Foreword by Jeffrey John
The former Dean of Divinity, Magdalen College, Oxford

This little book provides a simple structure with varied, inspirational content for a whole month's morning and evening prayer. The themes are carefully chosen to balance praise and penitence, personal devotion and intercession for others. The style is modern and natural, so that you can pray the prayers as your own without any self-consciousness. The author, the late Christopher Bunch, was Vicar of Otford, Diocese of Rochester, for twenty-eight years, and previously for ten years Vicar of Holy Trinity, Bromley Common.

ISBN 1-85311-059-0

Pilgrim Guide to the Holy Land Gospel Sites
NORMAN WAREHAM and JILL GILL
by Richard Third
Canterbury

A practical guide for the Christian visitor who wishes to 'walk in the footsteps of Jesus'. Bible references, chosen reading, factual details, and comments. Illustrated.

ISBN 1-85311-050-7

 # The Canterbury Press Norwich
The book publishing imprint of Hymns Ancient and Modern Limited
a registered charity
ST MARY'S PLAIN, NORWICH, NORFOLK, NR3 3BH
Telephone: (0603) 616563 and 612914   Fax: (0603) 624483